LET YOUR BODY WIN

STRESS
MANAGEMENT
PLAIN
& SIMPLE

JACQUELYN FERGUSON

WHOLE PERSON ASSOCIATES
DULUTH, MINNESOTA

Whole Person Associates, Inc.
210 West Michigan
Duluth, MN 55802-1908   218-727-0500
E-mail: books@wholeperson.com
Web site: http://www.wholeperson.com

Let Your Body Win: Stress Management Plain & Simple
Copyright © 2010 by Jacquelyn Ferguson

Printed in the United States of America

10   9   8   7   6   5   4   3   2   1

Editorial Director: Peg Johnson
Art Director: Joy Dey

Library of Congress Control Number: 2009927355
ISBN-13   978-1-57025-232-7
ISBN   1-57025-232-7

WHOLE PERSON ASSOCIATES
210 West Michigan
Duluth, MN 55802-1908

DEDICATION

To my parents
whose practicality, sense of humor
and commitment to personal responsibility
permeate all that is in this book.

CONTENTS

INTRODUCTION

Do you realize that if you had no stress at all you'd be dead? So stress itself isn't the problem. It's the quantity and quality of your stress and how you manage it that matters.

It has been estimated that today's adults live with approximately 100 times more stress than their great-grandparents! Even with this greatly increased amount of stress most of us have the resiliency to bounce back from our daily dose.

Research over the past several years is telling us that the real problem is chronic stress; elevated stress that goes on month after month, possibly year after year. Classic examples of chronic stress include the stress from catastrophic events such as hurricanes and their aftermath, long-term stress such as that experienced by caregivers, or a lifetime of hotheadedness.

We've known for decades that stress exacerbates illness and disease. More recently, however, many researchers have found that chronic stress can actually cause (or make you more vulnerable to develop) diseases: cardiovascular disease and diabetes, as well as depression. Additionally, stress is also connected to chronic fatigue syndrome, insomnia and irritable bowel syndrome, among many other disorders. In another decade or two they may find an association between chronic stress and many more physical and emotional problems that afflict humanity.

This is not to say that stress causes all things that go wrong with us. Nor am I suggesting that through better stress management you can cure yourself of anything that ails you. Let's never underestimate the power that your genes have in determining disease development. New research will continue to shed light on the negative consequences of too much stress and how to mitigate it.

It makes sense that your physical body pays the consequences of too much pressure because every time you're stressed your stress response, the fight/flight response, sets off a myriad of physical changes: a faster heart rate, muscle tension, the release of stress hormones and chemicals, etc. There's a lot of wear and tear on your heart and other organs. Tissues eventually break down where you have a genetic weakness and/or where you are vulnerable due to your lifetime of bad habits.

Your time of chronic stress will almost certainly come some day if you haven't experienced it already. If you're experiencing chronic stress now you need to follow stress management advice more faithfully than ever. Get into and stay in *Stress Shape* all of the time as an insurance policy so that you can have greater resiliency when chronic stress knocks on your door.

The purpose of this book

The purpose of this book is to help you understand that stress pushes you toward your *Stress Cliff*, the point where stress begins to damage you physically, mentally and emotionally. My hope is that you will begin to pull yourself back from your *Stress Cliff* by channeling your fight/flight energy in productive ways versus slamming on its brakes, which keeps the energy coursing through your physical system. The way that I'll encourage you to do this is through *Stress Breaks*. Some of these take only seconds while others require thirty minutes or more.

Included throughout this book are activities that can help personalize the information to your situation. You will be much more likely to act on this information if you complete the activities that are pertinent to the work you need to do.

What this book is not about

It's very important to understand that this book is not about the most important point in stress management: stress is in the mind of the beholder. How you behold or interpret situations in your life will determine whether or not you are stressed by them. The perception of stress is what triggers the fight/flight response in the first place.

For example, you and I have the same job and we're both being overworked. I see the situation as abusive and you see it as a challenge. Who has more stress? I do. This does not mean you're right and I'm wrong, it simply means that how I interpret the work conditions will determine the degree, if any, of stress I feel from them. In the long run, perhaps you will end up having more stress because as you keep doing the work you get more added to your pile, which could burn you out faster.

My interpretation of being abused on the job triggers my stress response more often making me more vulnerable to its consequences. In other words, vulnerability to the ravages of stress is determined to a huge degree by how you interpret your life's stressors (not to mention your genetics.) That's why some people can go through serious, chronic stress seemingly unscathed while others end up seriously ill.

By challenging your interpretation of events you open up new potential solutions to what stresses you, which can diminish your fight/flight response. This is the number one way to limit the harm stress does to you; the topic for another book.

For purposes of this book we'll consider the mostly physical consequences of your stress. We'll work to increase your awareness of how stress can make you sick and even kill you prematurely and what you can do to limit this damage.

CHAPTER 1

ALWAYS LET YOUR BODY WIN

VIRTUALLY EVERYONE KNOWS what they should do to reduce their stress, like exercise, relax, etc. But do you do these things on a regular basis? Most of us don't.

What most seem not to realize is why we need to take better care of ourselves. In a nutshell, it's because stress increases the risk that you will develop certain illnesses and diseases. It doesn't cause each and every illness out there but causes or contributes to many.

My mission

My mission in all the work I do is to inspire you to live a conscious life of personal responsibility in your relations with yourself and with others. What does this have to do with this book? Once you've read the following information you'll be more conscious of the fact that too much stress has physical, mental, and emotional consequences that virtually everyone suffers from. Possible symptoms of excessive strain include everything from headaches to insomnia, irritable bowel syndrome to developing diabetes or cardiovascular disease.

Your responsibility

Once you become consciously aware of the damage stress does to your body, you have two choices:

- Do something to mitigate the damage of stress.
- Do nothing different.

What I hope for you, of course, is that you will follow the advice in this and other stress reduction books to help you protect yourself from the physical and emotional ravages of anxiety and stress.

If you choose to do nothing different, then I at least encourage you to remain conscious of this choice. As you race through yet another very stressful day and are consciously aware that you choose to do nothing different, raise your right hand and say . . .

 *"I choose to send cortisol coursing through my system."*

Because, you see, it is predominantly cortisol, a fight/flight glucocorticoid hormone that in excess puts too much strain on your body. I focus on cortisol because it is the most potent of the glucocorticoids and makes up the majority of their activity. Plus, it's easier to pronounce. Additionally, its potentially harmful effects last much longer than the rev-you-up hormones (adrenalin and noradrenalin aka epinephrine and nerephinephrine.)

I'll work to keep you conscious about your choices and to drive home my message by repeating, "I choose to send cortisol coursing through my system" throughout the book.

Terms to look for in this book

Stress Cliff: the point at which stress begins to damage you physically, emotionally and/or mentally. It's different for everyone given the differences in genetics, health habits, etc. Once you reach your own *Stress Cliff* you can expect a growing number of symptoms and outright illness or disease to develop.

Stress Breaks: These are a multitude of ways to either release your stress energy (e.g., through exercise) or to relax it (e.g., through deep relaxation.) Any break from stress that works for you can be considered a *Stress Break*. The key to protecting yourself is to balance your stress with rest—rest away from your stress.

Stress Shape: When you use the quantity of *Stress Breaks* that pull you back from your own *Stress Cliff* you'll have yourself in *Stress Shape*. You'll be protecting yourself better from the ravages of stress.

Always let your body win!

My advice to you is to commit to always letting your body win out. What I mean by this is that your body, as well as your emotions, will give you plenty of warning when stress is accumulating and beginning to break down your physical and emotional systems. When you notice any physical and or emotional deterioration, make a commitment to yourself to protect yourself by following stress reduction advice. If you don't, your stress response can end up doing far more damage to you than the stressors themselves.

I have followed this axiom all of my adult life. Whenever I've noticed a physical symptom, such as headaches, I've changed whatever I thought was causing the symptom. For example, decades ago I was sure my headaches, which I rarely experienced, were from smoking, so I quit. (I know that's terrible to admit, but I did smoke when I was younger.)

So, right now, pledge to your mind and body that you will make healthier choices when a negative symptom appears or when an old symptom worsens. Do your best to identify which stressor in your life is causing it. A great way to do this is through the journaling technique found in Stress Break #4: write a letter from your body to yourself.

If you're not willing to make some of the more difficult decisions to change what you're doing, at least remain conscious that you choose to change nothing and remind yourself that you choose to send cortisol coursing through your system. Hopefully, someday, instead of saying, "I choose to send cortisol coursing through my system" you'll decide to make healthy changes that can help to balance this necessary, but in excess, dangerous hormone.

The easy part of stress management

What follows in this book is what I refer to as the easy part of stress management—techniques and exercises that minimize the negative, mostly physical consequences of stress. The difficult part of stress management is the mental component; how you perceive a situation, which determines whether or not you're stressed by it. Tackling the easy part of stress reduction can put you into better *Stress Shape* making you mentally and physically healthier to handle the more difficult aspects.

You know what you're supposed to do to lower your stress but do you know why?

We all know that we should meditate, exercise, eat a healthy diet, etc., etc., but do you know why? This book is motivated by the fact that most people in my workshops know what to do but they don't do it. Once they understand why they need to do healthier things they tend to get it.

So let's get on with the business of getting it.

CHAPTER 2

WHY STRESS CAN HURT YOU

YOU'RE DRIVING DOWN A BUSY HIGHWAY when suddenly another car cuts you off, almost causing an accident! You slam on your brakes! You scream obscenities at the other driver! Adrenaline is coursing through your system! Your heart is in your throat! Your hands are sweating and shaking!

This is your body in the fight/flight mode. It prepares you to defend yourself against any and all danger—real or perceived. All of your survival mental and physical systems are on high alert. Your vision and hearing are heightened; your muscles and vital organs are ready for any challenge you may encounter. But this physical state cannot go on forever.

The fight/flight response is key to understanding the consequences of stress

To understand the wear and tear of stress on your physical and emotional self you first have to understand the fight/flight response.

You've heard about the origins of it; all humans and most animals are equipped with this automatic and physical reaction to stress called the fight/flight response or the stress response. When you are stressed by anything, your heart beats faster, your breathing becomes shallow and your muscles tense. These are just a few of the physical changes that take place.

The more severe the stressor is, the greater the degree to which the fight/flight kicks in. For example, if you find yourself mildly aggravated by a minor stressor, such as a coworker who cracks her gum, you're not likely to notice the fight/flight kick in. But driving down the highway when someone almost runs into you and your heart's in your throat—well, that's noticeable.

The original intent of the fight/flight was to protect our ancestors from physical harm. When they came upon a wild animal or other danger their fight/flight response revved up their bodies to prepare them to either physically fight the danger or physically run away from it.

This protection was certainly important for our ancestors who struggled to survive in their sometimes hostile and very physical environment. The fight/flight worked better for them because they took their stress energy and actually physically acted on it. In other words, the energy was dispersed in the intended way—they physically fought or physically fled.

But most of today's stressors are mental, not physical, requiring mental not physical solutions. In today's world it's inappropriate to punch somebody out when you're stressed by them or to physically run away from them, so you have to slam on the brakes of your own stress energy.

But what happens to that energy? Does it just dissipate? Or does it put wear and tear on your physical body and your emotional self?

The correct answer, as we know from mounting research, of course, is that the constant triggering of the fight/flight response wears you down physically and emotionally. Even little hassles that aren't worth risking your health over contribute to the eventual accumulation of physical and emotional symptoms.

For example, your in-laws call. Just the sound of their voices sets you on edge. Do you realize that your stress response just ordered your stomach to diminish or even stop digesting? Because the fight/flight response is all about survival and digesting food is not essential to physically fighting or fleeing, it orders nonessential systems to shut down or slow down and essential physical survival systems to rev up. Could this have something to do with why so many people have digestive problems? The answer is yes. They are interrupting their digestive processes too often.

My own belief is that genetics and a lifetime of bad habits largely determine what will ultimately make you sick. Stress significantly influences when that will happen.

The other stress hormone: oxytocin

Psychologist Shelley Taylor of UCLA argues that the fight/flight response is more about what happens to men under stress than to women, who are generally less aggressive. Additionally, because women are responsible for taking care of the young she suggests that the female stress response is more about tend and befriend, making women more focused on caregiving and seeking out social support when stressed. The hormone oxytocin seems more connected to this response. Both sexes experience all of these hormones. There has been significantly more research done on the traditional fight/flight response.

But this book is about the glucocorticoids that, along with ephinephrine and norephinephrine, prepare your body for major physical expenditures of energy and the toll it takes on both sexes.

In the meantime, we'll have to wait for Taylor's fascinating research to be expanded and replicated to document the possible differences between the sexes in their responses to stress.

What are your present-day saber-toothed tigers?

Which stressors are you spending your vital energy on? Dealing with a difficult boss? Financial stress? Keeping up with change? Family conflicts? Traffic? Do customers, coworkers or kids push your buttons?

That's not to say that some of these stressors aren't worth your energy. However, read on and discover the possible consequences. The information will help you pick and choose which stressors are worth the energy that you're investing in them.

The triggering of your fight/flight in response to your stressors does no real damage if your body returns fairly quickly to a state of physical balance so it can recover from the energy drain. The danger is that today's fast-paced lifestyle triggers the fight/flight many times a day, if not an hour, leaving too many of us with an elevated stress response all day, day in and day out. If your body doesn't have time to recover from one triggering event to the next you end up in a near constant state of tension. This leads to exhaustion and irritability, to say the least, accelerates aging and eventually leads to illness and even disease.

If you were to take a science class on the physiology of the fight/flight response you could clearly see why too much stress takes its toll (more on this later). Here are some of the physiological changes that take place in your body every time you're stressed by anything.

In the table below you can see a glimpse of:

- What happens to your physical body each time you're stressed (left column).
- Its original purpose—it's always to protect you in times of potential danger (center column).
- The effect that prolonged stress can have on your body (right column).

PHYSICAL REACTION	SURVIVAL INTENT	LONG-TERM CONSEQUENCES
Blood leaves head, hands, and feet	Goes to muscles to prepare them for action	Cold hands/feet; headaches
Faster breathing	More oxygen to fight better or run faster	Chest pains from tired diaphragm muscles, faintness
Muscle tension	Prepares muscles for physical action	Fatigue, muscle ache
Faster heart rate	Pump blood faster	Elevated blood pressure
Extra insulin to transport sugars from the blood into cells	Greater energy	Low blood sugar level makes you feel tired; diabetes
Increased blood coagulation	Minimize blood loss in case of injury	Increased stroke risk
Digestion stops or slows down	Divert blood to large muscles	Digestive problems

"From a biological standpoint, the stress response can be considered as a shift from building or anabolic processes, to breaking down or catabolic processes," says Nick Hall, Ph.D. This is great for fighting and fleeing "but when there is a chronic shift from anabolic to catabolic processes, it can contribute to all sorts of disorders."

Not every stressor generates the exact same stress response. For a scientific explanation on why this is and for far more information on the stress response than you'll ever need, read Robert Sapolsky's *Why Zebras Don't Get Ulcers: An Updated Guide to Stress, Stress Related Diseases, and Coping,* 3rd Edition, published by Holt Paperbacks.

This all-too-human physical fight/flight reaction to stress is fascinating. For some reason I became aware of this physical phenomenon when I was in early grade school. At first, of course, it frightened me. But as I got older it began to intrigue me.

What was that burst of energy that shot through my body at times? What triggered it? Should I be afraid of it? What was its purpose? Did everybody experience it?

Decades later I became a stress management coach, international speaker and columnist on this subject. I learned that the fight/flight response was a normal physiological reaction to stress that we all have. For survival reasons we must always be ready to fight danger or flee from it. So far, so good.

Who's at greatest risk?

When the fight/flight begins to work against us is when you live with too much stress, too much of the time. Excessive physical changes triggered by the fight/flight lead to physical entropy, a lessening of energy available to you, unless you work to minimize the danger.

The three most vulnerable groups to the ravages of the stress response and who most need to take preventative action are:

- Those experiencing chronic stress.
- Those caught up in the runaway American lifestyle.
- Hotheads with too much impatience and hostility.

Some day your body will present its bill to you

The research is mounting that if you have enough stress in your life your body will someday present its bill to you. The American Institute of Stress has a list of 50 common signs and symptoms of the effects of stress and a diagram showing the effects of stress on different parts of the body. They note that 75% to 90% of visits to primary care physicians are for stress-related complaints. (http://www.stress.org/Effects_of_stress.htm.)

The situations listed below are most likely to produce negative physical effects. If any of these describe your present or recent stress profile, you'll need to put serious effort into immediate and on-going stress reduction.

- On-going stress, especially if it's beyond your control, and stress in more than one major area of your life: for example, high demand and low control at work plus a stressful family life.

- Persistent stress following a serious or traumatic event such as a car accident: after traumatic events watch for physical or emotional changes in yourself whether or not you believe they are related to the event.

- Too much activity and too little rest over too long a period of time (too true of most Americans, especially parents).

- On-going stress along with a serious disease, like diabetes: if you suffer from a major disease it is especially important that you practice excellent stress reduction techniques.

Possible consequences of too much stress

Everyone develops stress symptoms differently. Some people show their stress mostly through physical problems while others exhibit theirs through bad habits, which can lead to physical problems. Here is a list of some of the warning signs that you are under enough stress to be paying consequences. Which of these do you experience? (A more complete list is found in Chapter 4.)

Physical signs of stress such as
- headaches
- back pain
- indigestion
- chronic fatigue syndrome
- fibromyalgia

An increase in any bad habit such as
- nail biting
- smoking
- over/under eating
- drinking
- sleeping
- abusing drugs
- hair twirling/pulling
- excessive TV watching

Emotional and mental symptoms such as
- depression
- panic attacks
- road rage
- obsessive worrying

Which of these many symptoms do you exhibit on an increasing basis?
Take the Symptoms Assessment in Chapter 4 to help you determine the
degree to which stress is affecting you.

CHAPTER 3

CORTISOL'S EFFECTS ON HEALTH

Take a moment right now to rate your own health. Do you think your ongoing health is:

Excellent   Very Good   Good   Fair   Poor

How you just rated your health can predict your future regarding disease and longevity more accurately than your most thorough medical records.

This finding is from fascinating 2006 research that appeared in the Journal of Behavioral Medicine. It makes sense since you live with yourself 24/7. Just as when you drive the same car for a long time you know when something's off, you also know when you're off; when you're not sleeping well or you're constipated.

The researchers found that people who considered themselves healthy experienced a wider fluctuation of the fight/flight response when it kicked in. Since they aren't normally overly stressed it's more noticeable when it's triggered.

Those who rated themselves unhealthy didn't notice when their fight/flight kicked in as much.

Think about this because it points to what's damaging us. If you have elevated stress (and so more likely to have rated your health as fair or poor) you have an elevated fight/flight response much of the time. Over time you can adapt to how stress physically feels to the point where it feels normal to you. Your new normal can build slowly. A year or more down the road you find you have gradually accumulated more and more physical symptoms.

Dr. Robert Sapolsky, in his book, *Why Zebras Don't Get Ulcers*, explains the essence of what stress does:

> No single disastrous effect, no lone gunman. Instead, kicking and poking and impeding, here and there, make this a bit worse, [make] that a bit less effective. Thus making it more likely for the roof to cave in one day.

Listen to your body and your emotions every day and integrate **Stress Breaks** into your daily routine to avoid many—if not most—of these deteriorating symptoms and illnesses.

What is cortisol and why does it hurt you?

Cortisol is one of the many hormones released whenever your fight/flight is triggered. It's produced by your adrenal glands in response to the stress you perceive and is considered the primary stress hormone. (I focus on cortisol versus the other stress hormones because it is longer lasting and has a greater impact on your blood glucose and immune systems causing more emotional and physical damage.)

Two of cortisol's primary functions are:

- To help regulate your wake/sleep cycle.
- To tell the brain to eat after the exertion of fighting or fleeing. This was a necessary function to restore energy that our physically active ancestors truly needed, but our nonphysical reactions to stress don't require. This causes much of our problem.

A small amount of cortisol is required for your body to function normally. Too much cortisol coursing through your system leads to everything from insomnia to diabetes. An excess of it weakens your health over time, when your body isn't able to relax and recover sufficiently from stress.

According to Dr. Shawn Talbott, associate professor with the University of Utah's Department of Nutrition and author of *The Cortisol Connection*, "Chronically elevated cortisol levels lead to adverse effects on diverse body systems, including muscle and bone loss, fat gain, elevated blood sugar, high blood pressure, suppressed immune system function, and changes in memory and mood."

Phew! In other words, cortisol affects your overall physical functioning as well as your moods!

Cortisol and all of the other fight/flight hormones triggered are intended to protect you from physical harm by allowing you to better fight or flee from danger. But too much of these hormones over a long period of time is damaging.

The fight/flight response worked better for our ancestors than it does for us because of two major differences between us:

First, our ancestors' stressors had a more definitive beginning and ending, for example, hunting a wild animal. Today we have more continuous stress like traffic and deadlines.

Second, our ancestors, through literal fighting and fleeing, used up their stress energy far more than we do today. Given that most modern stressors are mental, such as getting along with people, and not physical dangers, such as protecting our families from wild animals, our stress energy just floats around accumulating in our blood and tissues. We send cortisol coursing through our system without releasing it through physical activity. To add insult to injury, we make this imbalance worse by neglecting to get enough rest.

These differences explain why the fight/flight hormones (particularly cortisol) are more harmful to modern humans. Too much stress keeps your body on high alert and is the main cause of stress-related health problems.

Whether or not your stressor requires you to physically fight or run, cortisol is released, saturating your body. Consider this: every time you're aggravated by your coworker who cracks his knuckles, or your children when they don't clean their rooms to your standards, or your boss who criticizes you too much, you release stress hormones. Just thinking about these life abuses sends a multitude of chemical changes throughout your system.

Triggered by your perception of stress, your brain activates your pituitary gland to release a chemical known as ACTH, which stimulates the adrenal gland to produce and release cortisol. For many people it runs most of the time, rarely shutting down, dangerously affecting their physical health.

If you belong to any one or more of the three groups I've identified as being the most vulnerable to the ravages of stress (those with chronic stress, too much impatience/hostility, or those caught up in the runaway American lifestyle) you may have too much cortisol coursing through your system.

The challenge is to balance this important hormone in your system. You want just enough to function well but not so much that you suffer from its negative consequences.

Cortisol is also related to depression and fatigue

Elevated cortisol also contributes to depression while too little secretion is related to chronic fatigue syndrome (CFS) according to Drs. George Chrousos, Chief of the Pediatric and Reproductive Endocrinology Branch at the National Institute of Child Health and Human Development, and Philip Gold, of the Clinical Neuroendocrinology Branch at the National Institute of Mental Health.

Their theory holds that the hormonal system known as the hypothalamus-pituitary-adrenal (HPA) axis, sets off a complex series of events that take place when you're stressed.

The HPA axis is a feedback loop where the brain signals the release of hormones needed for the fight/flight response. It affects the:

- Autonomic nervous system (controls heart rate, digestion, etc.).
- Limbic system in your brain (controls mood).
- Brain's amygdala (generates fear in response to danger).
- Hippocampus (involved in memory formation, in mood and motivation).
- Brain regions that control body temperature, suppress appetite, and control pain.
- Glandular systems producing reproductive, growth, and **thyroid** hormones.

According to Dr. Chrousos, the HPA axis varies from person to person and is probably influenced by heredity. In most people it functions well, appropriately responding to a threat and switching off when the threat is over. Others, however, under- or over-react.

With major stressors in early childhood, the HPA axis feedback loop becomes stronger with each new stressful experience. By adulthood this can produce an extremely sensitive stress circuit where the person overreacts hormonally to comparatively minor situations. In other words, the person has a short fight/flight fuse and even minor threats can trigger a seemingly too-strong reaction.

It's largely accepted that chronic stress and the subsequent cortisol releases are related to depression. Cortisol is produced in excess in depressed people and has a toxic effect on the hippocampus. Chrousos finds that people with depression can turn on the fight/flight response, but can't turn it off again, producing constant anxiety and overreaction to stimulation. This can be followed by learned helplessness: they give up trying to improve.

Some neuroscientists believe that the major changes in serotonin and other neurotransmitters seen in depression are not the cause of depression, but a reaction to the stress response.

Chronic fatigue syndrome is also generally accepted as a stress-related disease and a dysfunction of the HPA axis but with lower levels of cortisol. Those with difficulty sleeping had higher cortisol levels in the evening. (Learning deep relaxation techniques found in Chapter 11 is helpful in lowering the cortisol to enhance sleep.)

Dr. Chrousos advises that chronic stress shouldn't be taken lightly or accepted as a fact of life. "Persistent, unremitting stress leads to a variety of serious health problems. Anyone who suffers from chronic stress needs to take steps to alleviate it . . . by learning to relax and calm down."

To minimize your own mounting physical problems consider that stress management can be as important as any medication you take. It's in your best interest to take this information very seriously; the sooner the better for your mental and physical health.

Cortisol and weight gain ties debated

Cortisol has become the newest excuse for packing on the pounds. However, the research jury is still out on whether high levels of cortisol actually cause weight gain.

The minimum that seems to be true is that since one of the roles of cortisol during stress is to provide your body with energy, it can cause an increase in appetite. In other words, stress might lead you to eat more.

"During the first couple of days following a stressful event, cortisol is giving you a cue to eat high-carbohydrate foods," says endocrinologist Ricardo Perfetti, M.D., Ph.D., of Cedars Sinai Medical Center in Los Angeles. "Once you comply, you quickly learn a behavioral response that you can feel almost destined to repeat anytime you feel stressed."

Stress hormones, including epinephrine (the U.S. term for adrenaline) which gives you instant energy, as well as corticotrophin releasing hormone (CRH) and cortisol, provide the biochemical energy you need to fight or flee your stressors. High levels of epinephrine and CRH decrease appetite at first for a short time. Cortisol helps replenish your body after the stress has passed, and lasts longer.

The problem, according to Dr. Talbott, is that, "Too often today's response to stress is to sit and stew in our frustration and anger, without expending any of the calories that we would if we were physically fighting our way out of stress or danger (as our ancestors did)."

Your body doesn't know that you're not physically fighting or fleeing, so it still responds to stress with the hormonal signal to replenish nutritional stores. This makes you feel hungry, and the resultant extra eating may cause weight gain.

Dr. Perfetti tells us the fuel your muscles need during the fight/flight response is sugar, and that is why you crave carbohydrates when stressed.

Abdominal fat

Another unresolved research question is whether elevated cortisol causes fat to deposit in your abdominal area. Some research shows that abdominal fat causes certain chemical changes that can cause lower metabolism and increase cravings for sweets, possibly leading to even more weight gain.

Add more stress, therefore more cortisol, and less physical activity and you've got the necessary ingredients for heart disease.

However, Mayo Clinic dietitian Katherine Zeratsky, RD, LD, finds no evidence that the amount of cortisol produced by a healthy person under stress is enough to cause weight gain. She says that stress creates high levels of cortisol in your system causing you to accumulate excess fat only when your body produces large amounts of cortisol due to side effects of medication or an underlying medical condition like Cushing's syndrome. Dr. Caroline Cederquist is a board certified family and bariatric physician who works with patients with abdominal weight issues. She believes our high stress life styles create cortisol-induced symptoms, including abdominal weight gain. It can also lead to higher cholesterol and blood sugar levels and elevated blood pressure, all factors for heart disease.

Whether stress hormones or habits or a combination of both cause your increase in weight, research shows that there are ways to interrupt the cycle and stop the weight gain. Notice how the advice is the same as it is for living a healthier lifestyle. (There is much more detailed information on some of these in later chapters.)

- Relieve your stressors or cope more effectively with them.

- Exercise to burn calories and to produce a variety of biochemicals that counter the negative effects of the stress hormones. As little as 20 minutes of exercise a day, three to five days a week, helps control your insulin and sugar levels. Be careful, though, because too much exercise can raise your cortisol levels and increase your stress.

- Eat a balanced diet and don't skip meals. Eat six small versus three large meals a day and include foods from all the food groups. This helps to balance your blood sugar levels inhibiting insulin production and reducing cortisol levels, all helping to control appetite and weight.

- Get enough sleep. When you don't, cortisol levels rise, increasing your hunger.

- Relax. Much like exercise, relaxation produces brain chemicals that counter the effects of stress. Whether you do yoga, deep breathing, or meditation multiple times a week, do whatever reaches that sea of calm that's within you.

- Snack on whole-grain, high-fiber foods versus the typical American habit of high sugar and simple-carbohydrates like cookies, crackers and chips, which increase insulin levels, increasing stress hormones, making you feel hungrier. Cereals like oatmeal or multi-grain flakes, along with fruits, help keep your insulin levels in check, which help control blood sugar levels and ultimately, hunger.

- Avoid caffeine, cigarettes and alcohol because these can cause stress and cortisol levels to increase, and blood sugar to drop, which spurs hunger.

- Take vitamins regularly since stress depletes the B-complex and Vitamin C, and possibly calcium and magnesium. These nutrients help balance the effects of cortisol and may even play a role in burning fat, so take a good multi-vitamin supplement.

If you're experiencing chronic stress, don't go on a strict diet. Canadian researchers found that severely limiting calorie intake can kick off a series of biochemical events that ultimately increase stress. This can make you feel hungrier.

The research on the role of cortisol in obesity is still speculative. Blaming your weight gain on stress ignores the fact that you may have developed a habit of eating in response to stress, which is a learned habit, encouraged by brain chemistry that can be unlearned.

Here's the bottom line about weight loss. It always has been the bottom line, which suggests it always will be—until a miracle weight loss treatment is invented. There are two ways to lose weight, eat fewer (and better) calories or burn more of those calories by moving your body more. It's truly that simple.

Future research should settle the question of the connection between cortisol and weight gain. In the meantime, the best thing to do is lower your stress and include many of the *Stress Breaks* found in following chapters into your daily and weekly routine.

To limit cortisol's damage, the trick is to create a balance between activity and rest.

To limit the potential damage from cortisol, the trick is to balance your stress with rest. Your rest habits strongly influence the negative consequences of your stress. Rest away from your stress could include time out to work on a hobby or literal rest like a nap. The more stressed you are, and the more you're already paying a physical or emotional price, the more important to your health it is to schedule multiple *Stress Breaks* throughout each day.

In the next chapter we will assess how vulnerable you personally are to the physical and emotional consequences of too much stress.

CHAPTER 4

HOW VULNERABLE ARE YOU?

EVERYONE EXPERIENCES SYMPTOMS of stress from time to time. As long as your stress remains acute you are probably safe from its more serious consequences. However, once you enter the realm of chronic stress, hotheadedness, or have too many years invested in the runaway American lifestyle, you set yourself up for an accumulation of symptoms that can develop into something more serious.

Take the following Stress Symptom Assessment to determine your risk of developing illness, disease, or depression from the stress in your life. This is not a validated test but will give you a general idea of your level of risk.

Stress Symptoms Assessment

Directions: Check all of the following symptoms that you experience and the frequency with which you've experienced them:

> 0 = never/virtually never
>
> 1 = infrequently (e.g. more than once but not monthly)
>
> 2 = sometimes (e.g. monthly)
>
> 3 = frequently (e.g. 1–2 times/month)
>
> 4 = regularly (e.g. weekly or more)

SYMPTOM	0	1	2	3	4
Physical Symptoms					
1. Abdominal discomfort					
2. Allergies					
3. Back pain					

SYMPTOM	0	1	2	3	4
4. Blood pressure increase					
5. Shallow breathing					
6. Chest pain					
7. Cold hands or feet					
8. Cold sores					
9. Constipation					
10. Diarrhea					
11. Digestion problems					
12. Dry mouth					
13. Fatigue					
14. Feeling faint					
15. Frequent urination					
16. Gas, belching, burping					
17. Hair loss					
18. Headache, including migraine					
19. Heart palpitations					
20. Itching skin					
21. Menstrual irregularity					
22. Muscle tightness/spasms					
23. Nausea					
24. Pounding heart					
25. Skin problems: acne, eczema or other					
26. Startle easily					
27. Sweaty palms					
28. Teeth grinding					
29. Trembling					
Illness & Disease					
30. Cardiovascular disease (score 4 if you have it)					
31. Chronic Fatigue Syndrome (score 4 if you have it)					
32. Diabetes (score 4 if you have it)					
33. Fibromyalgia (score 4 if you have it)					
34. Irritable Bowel Syndrome					

SYMPTOM	0	1	2	3	4
Dietary Symptoms					
35. Increased appetite					
36. Craving for carbohydrates					
37. Decrease in muscle mass & increase in body fat					
38. Decrease in bone density					
Emotional & Mental Symptoms					
39. Anger, irritability					
40. Anxiety					
41. Concentration/focus problems					
42. Conflicts with others					
43. Confusion					
44. Crying					
45. Depressed or feeling down					
46. Fear					
47. Hopelessness/pessimism					
48. Insomnia					
49. Negative/pessimistic thinking					
50. Nightmares					
51. Panic attacks					
52. Sexual problems (loss of interest)					
53. Suicidal thoughts/attempts					
54. Withdrawal from friends/family					
55. Worry obsessively					
Increase in Bad Habits					
56. Biting fingernails/lips					
57. Drug and/or alcohol abuse					
58. Eating; either over or under-eating					
59. Hair pulling/twirling					
60. Sleep; either too much or too little					
61. Smoking					
62. TV watching					
Total each column					
Grand Total (All columns)					

Scoring: 0–248 possible score

0–70: Your stress appears relatively low and manageable. Everyone experiences some symptoms of stress at times, so don't worry—yet.

71–140: You're getting signals that your stress is mounting. Pay attention to what your body, emotions, and habits are telling you and do more serious stress reduction to keep your score from going higher.

141–190: WARNING! You're probably experiencing chronic stress. If you don't take better care of yourself you can expect to get sick more frequently and are at risk for disease development. You must begin serious stress reduction starting with the exercises in this book. Check with your physician for other options.

191–248: DOUBLE WARNING! Don't underestimate the damage that stress is doing to you. Begin seriously doing all of the exercises in this book regularly and check with your physician for other recommendations.

If you knew that stress management could alleviate or possibly even eliminate some of your health problems, would you be willing to do some things differently?

Notice your personal symptoms to know what's causing your stress

To increase your awareness of what's causing your stress, pay attention when your stress symptoms kick in:

- Notice what is going on around you. Do your stress symptoms get triggered when you are with certain people or doing certain things? Tom, an IT manager, noticed his blood pressure went up when he performed one part of his job and it went down when doing another. What does that tell him? Is there a way he could spend more of his time on the area of his work that lowered his blood pressure and less time on the area that increased it? Or could he think of ways to make the part of his work that increased his blood pressure less stressful?

- Watch yourself exhibiting your stress symptom. (This is called mindfulness or the observing self.) For instance, if you express your stress through over-eating, observe yourself when you over-eat. Don't try to change this behavior, just observe it. (The awareness you gain is a huge help in changing at some point.) Susan, a coaching client, observed herself overeating for a month. It put her much more in touch with the stressors that were triggering her over-eating reaction. Her main trigger was phone calls from her parents.

- Tune into your thinking. Wherever your thoughts are going is where you are going. Howard worried a lot about money. He noticed an increase in his drinking when he worried. This told him that he needed to take action to problem solve on his financial problems.

- Notice what you complain about the most. What do you dread? These areas are begging for your problem solving attention. The more you complain, the more stressed you are. Either problem solve about these issues or say to yourself, "I choose to send cortisol coursing through my system" every time you complain and do nothing. Eventually, saying this to yourself will wake you up to the damage the cortisol and other stress hormones are doing to you. One day you will actually do something about the problems at the source of your complaint.

- Tune into your body: What drains your energy? Which situations trigger anxiety reactions in you physically, like indigestion or a headache?

The first step in any change is to increase awareness. Pay attention to what's going on within and around you when you notice your stress symptoms. As your stressors become more apparent you can begin to open up your mind to problem-solving options. Options equal a sense of greater personal control. Having more personal control lowers your stress, which reduces the cortisol coursing through your system, which diminishes or eliminates your stress symptoms.

Listen to Your Body

Your body never lies to you. It will tell you when you're too stressed and need to slow down. Make a commitment to yourself that when you notice your body acting up in some way that you will listen to it and do whatever is necessary to fix what's stressing you. This is particularly important when a physical or emotional symptom persists or worsens.

For instance, Janice, a former coaching client with three children, noticed after significant challenges with one of her kids that she was having digestion problems—and this is a person who had a cast-iron digestive tract. Once she made the connection between her physical symptoms occurring when the conflict with her child erupted, she put her foot down to do what was necessary to solve the problem. After making the tough choices to resolve this issue, her stomach went back to normal telling her she had made a healthy choice.

Gradually increase your awareness of what is happening in your life when your body exhibits physical discomfort or you become ill. This will help you pinpoint the problem needing attention and resolution.

Stop and Reflect

Here's a great way to allow your body to communicate with you about what you need to do to pull back from your *Stress Cliff*. If you can do this now, please do. If not, remember to do it later. Before you begin, have paper and pen handy.

Sit comfortably and take a few deep breaths to relax. When you feel ready, close your eyes and scan your body slowly. Start by becoming aware of the top of your head, move down to your forehead and eyes, looking for any signs of discomfort, tension or pain. Continue focusing down through the rest of your face, your jaws, your head and down through your neck. Move into your shoulders and down through your arms and into your hands and fingers.

Notice your torso, both front and back, continuing to look for signs of discomfort. Move down through your hips, your legs and into your feet and toes.

Let your mind go back to just one part of your body that is particularly uncomfortable and focus on that discomfort for a moment.

If this part of your body could talk to you, what would it tell you to do to decrease your stress?

Write yourself a letter from the uncomfortable part of your body. Let it tell you what to do to make it feel better. Let the words flow without conscious effort. Don't force it. Just let it write itself.

Adapted from "Letter From the Interior," *Structured Exercises in Wellness Promotion Vol. 1*, Nancy Loving Tubesing, EdD and Donald A. Tubesing, MDiv, PhD, Whole Person Associates, Duluth, MN. www.wholeperson.com. 800-247-6789.

It was through this form of journaling that my coaching client discovered that she needed to resolve the conflict with her child and to stop denying the physical consequences she was suffering because of it.

After you write your letter, consider what it says. If you allowed the letter to write itself without real conscious effort on your part, you probably have received good advice on what to do. Now you just have to follow your own good counsel.

If you choose to do nothing to mitigate the damage of your stress then say to yourself,

 *"I choose to send cortisol coursing through my system."*

Every time you feel your symptom kick in repeat this to yourself over and over again. This will not only keep you conscious of your choices, it will also keep the responsibility for your lack of change right where it belongs: in your lap.

CHAPTER 5

VULNERABLE GROUP #1: CHRONIC STRESS

THE PEOPLE WHO ARE THE MOST VULNERABLE to the ravages of stress are those who have chronic stress. Most researchers would define chronic stress as elevated stress that lasts more than six months. Caregivers and those who've experienced serious catastrophes such as a hurricane and its aftermath qualify for chronic stress. Their stress goes on day after day, month after month, and, for some, year after year.

Chronic stress keeps the body on high alert and is the main cause of stress-related health problems. "If stress causes your blood pressure to go up, then chronic stress causes your blood pressure to go up chronically," says Dr. Robert Sapolsky. When your physical body is thrown into a state of imbalance each time the fight/flight kicks in, it needs to return to physical balance soon to restore its energy and to protect your health. But with chronic stress this doesn't happen often enough; thus the physical and emotional problems; thus the need for balance between rest and stress to protect yourself.

Acute stress is not what you have to worry about

Acute stress that triggers the fight/flight for a moment or even for hours over a day or more but then soon reverts back to normal is not likely to make you sick or kill you prematurely. Your body is able to restore its balance, therefore its energy, quite easily keeping you resilient to stress.

Over a typical lifetime most stress that is experienced is acute in that it comes and goes fairly quickly. This is not the stress you need to be concerned with unless you have health issues since even acute stress can exacerbate physical and emotional problems. Generally, however, most of us are capable of bouncing back after the normal day-to-day events. Humans are incredibly resilient and able to tolerate an unbelievable amount of stress.

Acute stress is represented below, with a state of balance represented by the horizontal line and the stress up-ticks, the vertical lines, lasting a short time. Examples of the up-tics in stress could be hassling with the kids or the morning traffic, an aggravating coworker interaction, with the longer lasting stress up-tick perhaps a meeting where your boss is coming down on everyone.

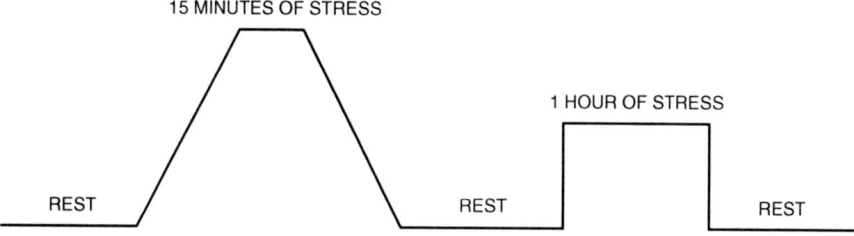

Acute stress may have sufficient rest in between bouts of stress. In the above example, the person's mind and body are able to rest and to prepare for the next stress up-ticks remaining quite safe from its ravages as long as this pattern continues. You're able to protect your resiliency for the next round.

More typical stress for most of us with hectic lives has the distribution of stress and rest looking more like this:

This pattern has more stress and less rest but is somewhat in balance. It has sufficient periods of rest in between stress upticks.

At least this pattern allows you to return to your previous level of rest.

Chronic stress is the scariest stress

Chronic stress should cause the most concern. This pattern has weeks/ months of stress with insufficient restoration of physical and emotional balance. With so much stress and so little rest, chronic stress leads to the physical and emotional negative consequences noted earlier.

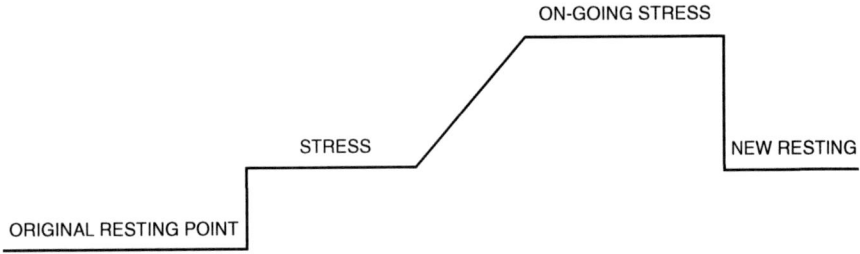

Notice in this pattern the new resting position is not as restful as the original.

An example of someone with chronic stress is Fred, a caregiver whose wife has had several hospitalizations and requires his care at home in between. Not only does his stress go up and stay up, his resting position is much higher than before the chronic stress began. In other words, it's not nearly as restful. Caregiving is often one stressor after another. The negative consequences keep mounting. Fred became ill himself after a few months of caring for his wife.

I intimately understand chronic caregiving stress; it's the only chronic stress I've experienced—so far. For the last year and a half of my parents' lives I was their primary caregiver. During this time I practiced excellent stress management: cardiovascular exercise three times/week, deep relaxation most days, hot baths multiple times/week (even though I didn't like them), weekly massages, eating a healthy diet, yoga, and getting good sleep. I delegated responsibilities to out-of-town siblings and asked for and got help when needed. About the only thing I didn't do was to take extra B vitamins.

Even when there were periods of relative stability with my parents' respective health problems, my resting level didn't go all the way down to my previous level, but to one that was lower than the chronic stress but higher than my previous resting level.

After the first year my chronic stress took a minor toll; I found that I no longer ran up stairs, which I'd done all of my life. I even remember not having enough energy to stretch before getting out of bed, another lifetime habit. How can you not have enough energy to stretch while lying down? It requires so little effort and produces such great results it's hard to imagine that I lacked the energy.

Shortly after both of my parents passed away (within less than three weeks of each other) my muscles were so tight I felt like I could break a bone doing nothing. My breathing became very weird and shallow. (It's interesting how you can hold up to the stress until it's over—then watch out for the consequences!) It took almost a year for these symptoms to go away. I got rid of them by continuing all of the healthy habits I'd always practiced, and adding Kripalu Yoga to my Hatha Yoga practices.

Imagine the physical problems I might have developed had I not taken such good care of myself before and during their illnesses.

Let your body win!

If you have stress in your life that resembles this chronic pattern, for the sake of your mental and physical health you need to dramatically change some of your habits to allow your energy to return to a state of balance as frequently as possible. You need to do your best to get your resting point to the healthier level it was before the chronic stress began.

I practiced all the *Stress Breaks* that are covered in this book long before my parents ever became ill. These good habits over the years found me in better *Stress Shape* so that I could better tolerate this period of chronic stress. During the year and a half of my caregiving I was even more faithful to my self-prescribed *Stress Breaks*—as I continue to be to this day. I believe this is why I suffered no physical illnesses during or after this period of intense stress.

Take chronic stress seriously

Chronic stress is a health concern because of the damage done to your body from the ongoing release of your fight/flight hormones, including cortisol. Remember that the fight/flight hormones were intended to protect our ancestors from physical harm, giving them the energy to either physically fight or physically run away from danger. But we don't tend to physically act on our fight/flight leaving the hormones coursing through our bodies looking for places to push to the limits.

According to accumulating research chronic stress can cause, not just exacerbate, at least two diseases: cardiovascular disease and diabetes. Again, if you study the biology of the fight/flight response, it would make sense to you why your body is vulnerable to developing these diseases.

In other words, chronic stress makes you more vulnerable to illnesses and diseases which can make you sick and ultimately can kill you.

The trick is to balance your stress with rest

Those who have chronic stress lack a vital balance in life, the balance between activity and rest. The trick, according to mounting research, is to balance your stress with rest.

Every single aggravation of your day triggers your fight/flight response and a corresponding anger/fear emotion (such as intimidation, fear, nervousness, exasperation, irritation, anger, impatience, etc.), making you more vulnerable to illness and disease.

So, limit the damage of stress by increasing your rest habits. The more stressed you are, and the more you're already paying a physical price for your stress, the more important to your health it is to schedule multiple *Stress Breaks* throughout every day. Regularly practice just seconds worth of deep breathing and get a full eight hours of sleep virtually every night. Self-prescribe your own *Stress Breaks* to reduce the damage of cortisol coursing through your system to get yourself into much better *Stress Shape*.

CHAPTER 6

VULNERABLE GROUP #2: THE RUNAWAY AMERICAN LIFESTYLE

AMERICA HAS A SICKNESS: it's the hurry-up sickness of our fast-paced 24/7, runaway American lifestyle. It speeds up more each year leaving me wondering what it'll be like in another generation. Giving in to this hectic lifestyle over the years can itself be considered chronic stress.

A classic symptom of America on overdrive, Nancy Shute wrote in *US News and World Report* in April 2007, "In the last three years alone, the number of 18 to 24-year-olds who drink coffee daily has doubled from 16% to 31% . . . Some of these young people also take prescription stimulants like . . . Ritalin for late-night study sessions. Energy drinks like Red Bull and Cocaine, with several times the buzz of a can of Coke, have mushroomed into a $3.5 billion a year industry."

No wonder our children feel the need to push themselves. They are over-scheduled in an attempt to get experience to prepare them for the reality of our hard-driving workplace.

Americans, in my opinion, work entirely too much. Did you know that we are the hardest working people in the industrialized world? Consider these statistics from the International Labor Organization, 2001:

- During the 1990s America's work year increased 36 hours to almost 49½ weeks a year, tracking greater productivity so we can buy more.
- America works more than any industrialized nation:
  2½ weeks more than Japan
  6½ weeks more than Britain
  12½ weeks more than Germany

We work entirely too hard and rest entirely too little.

♫ Slow Down You Move Too Fast ♫

Do you remember this line from the 1960s song by Simon and Garfunkel, *The 59th Street Bridge Song*? It's basically what we Americans need to do—slow down—to create more balance between activity and rest, which can pull us back from our *Stress Cliff*. To limit the damage that stress does to you you'll need to commit to doing multiple *Stress Breaks* every day to get yourself into better *Stress Shape* so you can better tolerate this crazy lifestyle.

Throughout the rest of the book, every so often, you'll see this musical note symbol ♫. Each time you see this I want you to sing in your head that opening line of this great song, "Slow down you move too fast."

The typical day of the average American

The following describes a typical day of the average American who's living in the rut of our runaway American lifestyle, adapted from writings by Joyce Case, a former colleague of mine.

> Your alarm blasts you out of your dreams. You can't believe it's already time to get up again. But you force yourself out of bed and stumble to the kitchen to put on the coffee. You hope to drink your morning wake-up coffee in peace when you hear your 13- and 11-year-olds fighting over bathroom rights. You mumble some peace-making advice and go back to get more coffee and perhaps a Danish.

> Later, as you are taking a shower while thinking about today's staff meeting, you notice the water rising above your ankles—again. You've got to remember to call someone to check that drain!

> You dress and go downstairs where you're told that the kids' ride for tonight canceled so you have to take them to their respective activities—on opposite sides of town. You make a mental note to leave work by 5:00 sharp to accommodate this change of plans.

> Your husband (or wife) calls down to ask where his blue suit is that you were to pick up at the cleaners. You tell him he looks great in gray and make another mental note—this time to pick up his suit.

> You gulp down one more cup of coffee; then it's off to your car, which starts—on the fifth try. You've got to get it in for a tune-up soon.

> You point your car in the right direction to do battle with rush-hour traffic, cell phone in hand. After cursing out a few drivers and fielding a couple of phone calls ♫ you arrive at work. Before heading to your office you stop

by to pick up another cup of coffee. Someone has brought in home-baked goodies that you know you shouldn't have but hey, you deserve it. It's going to be a stressful day.

In your office you push aside a stack of work left over from yesterday as you make your priority list for today. You have an hour-long staff meeting at 9:00, leaving you an hour to prepare for a meeting with your boss which begins at 11:00.

At 10:30 you finally conclude your staff meeting. You're feeling good, though, because your staff is on top of their responsibilities. There are four urgent phone messages waiting for you and you are able to get back to only one. That call produces several things to do and you begin doing some of them. Then you pull together information for your meeting with your boss, now only ten minutes away!

You rush to your boss's office for your meeting in which you look so organized and competent that he delegates even more to you. Great! It's just what you need ♫!

After the meeting you suddenly realize how hungry you are. You race out for a burger and a soda ♫. Back at your office you're warned that an irate customer is waiting for you. You soothe the savage beast and save another account for your company—as you nearly always do. You wonder if they're really aware of all that you do for them.

Then you return more phone calls, deal with dozens of emails. Your least favorite person bursts into your office. He's gloating over a battle he won and you lost. You tap your fingers as you listen so as not to attack him ♫.

Alone again, shaking, you go for another cup of coffee ♫. You work on some reports and plans interspersed with settling disagreements among your employees.

Before you know it, it is 5:20. You fly out the door and get into your race car to fight your way home. You stop at the grocery store to get things for dinner where you're tempted to ram other shoppers with your grocery cart because they are in your way and slow you down ♫.

Once home you and your husband throw dinner together while handling your kids without skipping a beat. After wolfing down dinner you fly through the kitchen to clean it up ♫. You're out the door with your kids and drop them off at their activities after which you go to a nearby park and finish some work on your laptop.

On the way home, the kids are fighting in the back seat and you yell at them to be quiet ♫. Don't they know you have a headache? Then the guilt sets in.

> At home you struggle to get the kids to do their homework and later to get them to go to bed before you finally flop down in front of the TV with a drink to help calm yourself before answering your email and going to bed.
>
> Before getting into bed you place your paper, pencil and flashlight beside your bed in case you wake up with inspirations about work. Writing these ideas down helps you get back to sleep more easily.
>
> You fall into bed and sleep fitfully—again, and wake up the next morning with the alarm blaring. You can't believe it's time to get up again.

How closely does this represent your life? It used to more closely resemble a mother's life, but increasingly it is all too familiar to fathers, as well.

This is also a description of rut living: you keep repeating the same behaviors day after day, month after month, year after year. Decades down the road you barely recognize the tired and cranky soul you've become.

Rut living is unconscious living; you don't think, you just do. If you're living in a rut, and if that rut contains too much stress that's harming you, think of the great quote from Dr. Susan Jeffers' book *Feel the Fear and Do It Anyway* written way back in 1988, but still valid today. "If you always do what you've always done, you'll always get what you've always gotten."

If you're not wild about the results of your rut life, you must do something different! Get conscious and become responsible for the changes. If you choose to do nothing different about your rut-living, at least consciously admit to yourself that you choose to keep its stress. Remember to say to yourself,

 *"I choose to send cortisol coursing through my system."*

Take heart and read on for ideas to reverse the damage of stress so you can have greater motivation to make other necessary changes that can give greater meaning and enjoyment to your life.

Technology contributes to the runaway American lifestyle

Technology contributes to this American illness with faster computers, e-mail, blackberries, fax machines, and cell phones with Internet access and text messaging.

What a world technology has created. It was supposed to make our lives easier and in some ways it has. Give me a word processor any day over a typewriter!

However, technology has also put our lives into overdrive. We race faster and faster. After a while it becomes normal. A bit longer and the pace becomes addictive. Eventually it can make us sick or kill us prematurely.

Ramped-up expectations ♬

One of the ways technology speeds up our lives is in our expectations that things will happen more quickly. When they don't, watch out! You tap your fingers when someone in a store is walking too slowly in front of you or you finish others' sentences. Your patience just isn't what it used to be.

For some, impatience grows into hostility ♬

Research has found that hostility leads to many health problems including diabetes and heart disease. Mix the hostility with interpersonal stress (hostility damages relationships, after all) and lowered self-esteem (hostility drives people away and is hard on your self-esteem) and you have a volatile mix for development of disease.

Technology also stresses us by keeping us electronically connected virtually all of our waking hours. Over time it can have the same effect as having small children. When you were a new parent do you remember how part of your brain stayed awake all night long? A few years of partial sleep left you exhausted. Being always connected electronically can have a similar effect. You're always on. You don't turn off. If you choose to stay ever-connected electronically, repeat after me,

 *"I choose to send cortisol coursing through my system."*

Do you wonder what this incredibly fast-paced life does to you?

The more hurried and stressed you are the more your fight/flight energy is triggered through a higher heart rate, increased muscle tension and epinephrine rushes. It's taking its physical toll on you.

When you get into the rut of speeding through life you seldom question the wisdom of what you're doing. You just try to cram more into each hour and day until something dramatic happens—like a heart attack!

Anything that speeds up your life too much needs to be altered in some way. Slow things down a little to reduce your stress.

- Insist upon certain hours of each day to be disconnected. Don't answer any phone. Let your emails mount up until tomorrow.
- Consciously slow down whatever you're doing at supersonic speed, whether it's talking, brushing your teeth or racing to beat the traffic light.
- Cut down on coffee and other stimulants.
- Slow down your driving speed by just 5 mph. You'll be amazed at how much more easily you'll go with the flow of traffic versus fighting it, trying to pass everyone to arrive a few seconds earlier.
- Deep breathe throughout your day whenever you feel stressed and s-t-r-e-t-c-h-e-d too thin.
- Get plenty of exercise, relaxation and sleep.

As a somewhat high-speeder myself, I've been doing these things for decades and they do help. Rather than being controlled by this American sickness, take charge and consciously create a bit slower pace to reduce your stress.

Even those who love high-speed need to balance activity with rest

The faster your lifestyle and the more stressed you are the more out of control you'll be and the faster you'll be careening toward your *Stress Cliff*. Even if you thrive on your fast-paced life style you still need to consciously balance all that you do with ways to rest yourself; anything that allows your fight/flight to be subdued, that allows your physical and mental self to be repaired and renewed. This will create a new energy balance in you so you'll have healthier energy to do the very things that are wearing you out!

Chapter 7

Vulnerable Group #3:
Anger, Hostility & Impatience

"Impatience is a fuse to a stress explosion," my husband once said. It can go off while standing in line at the grocery store or while navigating rush-hour traffic. People who irritate you or hold you up in some way can also be the detonation. For some, it can be ignited by pretty much anything.

Strong emotional reactions cloud your thinking

Have you ever noticed that when you are obviously stressed there is always an emotional component to your reaction? Anger and/or fear, Mother Nature's survival emotions, or any of their sub-emotions such as irritation, jealousy, loneliness, etc., are always present to the degree you perceive a threat (stress). These survival emotions were also originally intended to protect our ancestors from physical harm by triggering their fight/flight response.

When modern-day emotions are triggered they can make handling stress more difficult. Some people get lost in their emotions. Normal as this may be, at some point you need to move beyond the emotions to focus on solving the triggering problem if you expect to lower your stress.

Dr. Murray Brown, a systems theorist, says we have two inner guidance systems that determine our reactions.

- The first is most likely rooted in the deep limbic region of the brain. It is an automatic and instinctual reaction with emotional responses patterned from early life, including the fight/flight response.

- The second is mostly organized in the cerebral cortex, the newer evolutionary part of the brain that processes thought, reasoning, judgment and logic.

The more mature and the less stressed you are the more you can choose which side of your brain to operate from. A test of this is the degree to which you can calm yourself (when appropriate) and is indicative of your ability to use the cerebral cortex more.

Often when you are stressed, you believe that a person or situation is the cause. Generally, however, it is your interpretation of the event that is the true source of your stress. (Remember, stress is in the mind of the beholder.) When strong emotions are triggered, you may be reacting out of an automatic emotional response from early childhood. What you think is causing your stress may not be. When strong emotions inhibit relieving a stressor, ask yourself: "Who or what from my childhood could trigger this same reaction in me?"

For example, a man in one of my recent workshops was complaining very emotionally about his boss' management and communication styles. He couldn't understand why he reacted so automatically and defensively to his boss. I asked him the above question and he answered immediately and with surprise. His father, he said, triggered this same response in him. He recalled reacting very defensively to his father's parenting and communication styles, similar to his reaction to his boss.

In other words, this man's stress was not really caused by his boss. His boss simply triggered old emotional baggage from long ago.

This awareness can help him put his boss' style into perspective and help him reduce his resistance to him. If he were to journal his stressful thoughts and feelings about his boss (see Chapter 10), he could, with time, loosen the grip of his emotions and operate more out of the logical part of his brain.

When you react in an overly emotional way to a situation and find yourself unable to look at it with logic, unrelated feelings are probably clouding your perceptions. Journal them, talk to a non-judgmental person about them, meditate, or do whatever helps disperse your emotions. Then you'll be able to tap into your rational thinking brain sooner rather than later to reduce the stressor.

Don't let anger and/or hostility endanger your health

Hotheads, just like those with chronic stress, are at greater risk of at least cardiovascular disease and diabetes. Think about it: when you're consumed with road rage screaming insults at other drivers what do you suppose happens to your blood pressure? Elevated blood pressure over the years will take its toll. Don't fool yourself.

Someone who is often angry knows (at least if they're conscious) what anger feels like physically: increased heart rate, muscle tension, faster breathing, etc. It's that fight/flight response again, at the ready to defend you against any perceived wrong. (The key word here is perceived. If you don't perceive someone has wronged you, your fight/flight won't kick in.) Through your anger and impatience you choose to send cortisol coursing through your system! The trick is to know when your emotional response is worth the extra cortisol.

Do you have any of the main risk factors for heart attack and stroke?

_____ High blood pressure

_____ Obesity

_____ High blood cholesterol

_____ Are you a smoker?

If so, adding hostility and chronic anger to your symptoms could elevate that risk, or even prove fatal.

Even for those who don't have these risk factors, more and more of us are becoming increasingly impatient due to our incredibly stressful world of greater demands and hurried-up, instant technology expectations. For some, impatience grows into anger and hostility.

Our techno-stress-age with its accompanying expectations for everything to be faster can push even patient people to the edge ♫. However, for health reasons the concern is for those who are angry or impatient (a close cousin to anger) much of the time, often over insignificant events.

Anger is a normal emotion

Anger is perfectly normal as one of Mother Nature's survival emotions to motivate you to take appropriate action. Within the normal range it can motivate you. If you perceive an injustice your anger can motivate you to fight back . . . hopefully in an appropriate fashion, such as assertively speaking to your offender versus beating him up.

Too much anger, or inappropriately expressed anger, however, can be harmful to your relationships, not to mention your physical health.

Startling research: Do you think you're too young to worry about this?

Impatience and hostility are reactions to stress and are the damaging parts of the Type A personality because of the over-production of the stress response, including cortisol. Research has long shown that stress activates the sympathetic nervous system, causing narrowing of the blood vessels and an increase in blood pressure. These traits increase even a young adult's long-term risk of developing high blood pressure.

- According to a study funded by the National Heart, Lung, and Blood Institute and published by the Journal of the American Medical Association in 2003, 3,308 blacks and whites, ages 18 to 30 when the research began in 1985, were studied. It found that higher levels of impatience and hostility were significantly associated with the development of hypertension after 15 years. Greater amounts of impatience and hostility equated to a greater risk. Interestingly, competitiveness, depression, and anxiety didn't seem to increase the risk of hypertension.

  The subjects rated their time urgency/impatience. After 15 years, participants with the highest score had an 84% greater risk of developing high blood pressure! Those with the second-highest score had a 47% greater risk. What didn't affect the results: race, age, gender, education, blood pressure at the time of enrollment, or the presence of hypertension risk factors such as overweight/obesity, alcohol consumption, and physical activity.

- The famous Framingham Heart Study was performed under the direction of the National Heart Institute (now known as the National Heart, Lung, and Blood Institute). The study's objective was to identify the common factors or characteristics that contribute to cardiovascular disease (CVD). They followed its development over a long period of time in a large group of participants who had not yet developed overt symptoms of CVD or suffered a heart attack or stroke. Their findings suggested that those who experience frequent anger are more likely to have coronary artery disease and heart attacks. These people often have a hostile attitude toward life in general.

Are you enemy based?

Overly angry people can be enemy based. They look for and find enemies, even where there are none. They may interpret someone's nonverbal behavior as hostile when there was no such intent at all. They'll react to life's situations with anger, cynicism, mistrust and aggression. Enemy based people tend not to see themselves as such. If you've often been told you're a hothead you may very well be enemy based. Road rage is a classic example of enemy based perceptions.

If you become easily angered by traffic I bet you're blaming all those rotten drivers around you for a myriad of sins. And you, like many hotheads, probably enjoy the high of your own epinephrine, so feel little motivation to curb your temper. Here are more reasons you may want to reconsider.

- The greatest risk factor that contributes to strokes is hypertension, or high blood pressure. Given that those who are impatient, and by extension angry (since these two emotions are related) are at risk of higher blood pressure, this leads me to assume that impatience and anger are also contributors to strokes.

- Anger prone people (both men and women) are three times more likely than the least anger prone to have a heart attack or sudden cardiac death.

- Research on female-only subjects suggests that anger and hostility alone are not predictive for coronary artery disease in women, but women who outwardly express anger may be at increased risk if they also have other risk factors such as age, history of diabetes or levels of fats (lipids) in the blood. Cardiologist C. Noel Bairey Merz, M.D., medical director of the Preventive and Rehabilitative Cardiac Center and of Women's Health at Cedars-Sinai Medical Center, said the overt expression of anger toward others or objects appears to be the most toxic aspect of hostility in women. The researchers analyzed other measures related to anger including cynicism, hostility, aggression, and suppressed anger. Only expressed anger had a predictive value, and only in combination with another risk factor mentioned above.

- A recent study in *Circulation* found that hostility might increase the risk of death from cardiovascular disease in men with other risk factors.

- Dr. Nick Hall, a medical scientist, reports that discomfort with negative emotions, especially anger, correlates with increased susceptibility to some cancers and immune system dysfunction like rheumatoid arthritis.

In other words, excessive anger is bad for your health, not to mention your relationships.

When you couple hostility and anger with low control over a period of time, for instance staying in a bad marriage, you're inviting poor health by continually sending cortisol coursing through your system.

No matter what's triggering your frequent anger the most important element in taming it is to want to. Once your motivation is conscious there are many potential avenues for reining it in. Anger management could be beneficial to anyone with chronic anger and a hostile interpretation of life. Your body will be eternally grateful.

Victims and excessive blaming and complaining

People who see themselves as victims usually have a very high level of anger and hostility and, therefore, are very stressed. In fact, victims are the most stressed out people of all because they see no options other than to wait for the victimizer to treat them better. But the victimizer is beyond their control. Waiting for change can take forever.

Victims usually fit into the learned helplessness category (a condition coined by Dr. Martin Seligman of the University of Pennsylvania and author of *Learned Optimism*). They have learned to be helpless. They don't see other options except for the victimizer to somehow improve; they're powerless, which is an extremely stressful position. Any individual (or group of people) who excessively blames and complains about whomever or whatever is a victim. Victims tend to blame outside forces for their problems and for the lack of solutions, wasting massive amounts of energy. Blaming and complaining are typical victim pastimes.

It's easy to complain about or blame someone for stressing you. A certain amount of this is normal and can be beneficial if used for venting to enable you to move on to problem solving. The highly stressful blaming and complaining I'm referring to is the type that goes on and on and on and on—and on. Get the picture?

For instance, Evan is virtually always late getting his reports to Kari. This drives her nuts! She complains to others, "Why does he have to be late all the time? He's so disrespectful of me. He's always making me miss my deadlines."

A little complaining is normal but it becomes harmful when it goes on and on indicating that she is a victim and therefore powerless.

Do you complain about some things or people week after week, month after month, possibly even year after year? Most of us do. If so, you are a victim to whatever or whomever it is you're complaining about and you're sending cortisol coursing through your system. If you wait for the other person to change you'll be waiting for a very long time for your relief. Victims experience a lot of frustrating waiting.

Stop and Reflect

Be a Conscious Victim

Write a list of what you frequently complain about and for how long you've complained about it in terms of weeks or months:

COMPLAINT	HOW LONG?

If you've been complaining about something over time without changing your response to it, you've probably become a victim of the complaint. These situations become very stressful because you have learned to be helpless about them. You must look for viable options to deal with each more effectively to reduce this stressor. Read on.

Individuals and groups of people who truly have been victimized historically need to go through a process.

- They must become aware that they have been victimized.
- This awareness rightfully generates anger toward the people abusing them.
- Finally they need to move beyond the anger and take personal responsibility to improve their lives in ways that are within their control.

Let's use child abuse as an example. It's typical that children of abuse initially believe that they're to blame for it; somehow they deserve it and thusly they see themselves as unworthy and unlovable. At some point, if they're lucky, they see that they truly have been victims and their anger and indignation are rightly triggered and focused on the abuser. This stage of anger is very appropriate and healthy.

If the abused child (even if an adult by the time they realize they were abused) stays in the angry mode, however, continually blaming the abusers, they remain victims to them and remain powerless.

To reclaim their lives they must move through and then beyond anger. Many seek professional help through this very difficult stage.

(Those who have lived as a victim over multiple years may also qualify as having chronic stress leaving them vulnerable to illness and disease.)

Another example comes from the Women's Movement when many women worked through their anger through consciousness raising groups, where they discussed their own unequal status in a society that victimized them by tolerating physical abuse, unequal pay, etc. Lots of anger as well as humor were expressed in these gatherings. Expressions of these feelings helped countless women understand that females historically have been and still are victims of an unfair system. This raised their consciousness, "Yes! You have abused me!" was very freeing to victims, especially those who were still in the self-blame mode.

The resulting anger and the expression of it through demonstrations and political involvement were empowering for many women. Their growing sense of personal power motivated many to use their angry energy to take control to improve their own lives. There is evidence of this everywhere today. Those who remain in the blaming and complaining mode remain stuck in their pasts and victims to the system that pays them little attention.

Taking personal responsibility to make changes that are within your control is the antidote to being a powerless victim. If you're stuck in victimhood take the at-first bitter pill of personal responsibility and move on. The bitterness turns into sweetness in direct proportion to the degree to which you take charge of your own life.

Move beyond anger to reclaim your power

To work your way out of the victim mode:

- Be conscious: Consciously observe your blaming and complaining. Don't try to stop it or change it. Just observe it. You may do it out of habit. When you feel helpless it can just pop out. You may be totally unaware that you are even doing it. It's an unconscious reaction. Ask loved ones whom you trust to let you know when you're doing it. Then pay attention and become more conscious of it, the first step to changing it.

- Consciously accept responsibility for doing nothing: The only thing within your control is your reaction to everything. Complaining and blaming are reactions you choose.

 *"I choose to send cortisol coursing through my system."*

If you accept responsibility at a conscious level for this, it can eventually help you make other choices.

For example, once Kari becomes aware that she is a victim to her coworker, Evan, she needs to consciously say to herself when she blames him and complains about him, "I choose to be a victim to him." This very act of increasing her consciousness can hasten the day when she chooses to take charge and do something different!

Be proactive and identify your options: You could choose to be proactive rather than remaining reactive as victims tend to do. If Kari wants to get the reports on time and she continues to wait for Evan to get them to her, she could die before he becomes prompt. So she needs to do something different. She could start by figuring out her options. If she doesn't see any, she could enlist the help of a trusted person who is good at problem solving. A hint here: her solution will include an assertive response from her to him.

The best antidote to stress is seeing and acting on your options for solving a problem. Victims see no options except that the other person should change. Become conscious of your victim position and make a conscious choice to change it. Proactively consider your options and go for a solution. Or, at a minimum, be a conscious victim.

Learn self-soothing techniques

If you experience a great deal of time urgency, impatience and/or anger, you need to decide if hypertension is too high a price to pay. If it is, you'll need to learn patience. To help you do this you must learn to develop self-soothing techniques.

Impatience, as any form of anger, pushes you to look for the cause outside of yourself, like the *!★~ who cut you off in traffic. But this implies that the other person has to get out of your way for you to be soothed. Since that person is beyond your control you'll instead need to soothe yourself.

Self-soothing techniques to decrease anger:

- Deep breathe every time you find yourself becoming impatient (see Chapter 10).
- Distract yourself when impatient. For example, while standing in a checkout line read the sensationalist and comical tabloid headlines. They crack me up!
- Ultimately you must change how you interpret whatever is getting in your way. Learn to recognize your impatient interpretations, "You ignorant moron!" Instead invent your own self-soothing-interpretation such as, "How important will it be in one year that this person is slowing me down?" More often than not you'll answer, "It's not at all important. Why am I wasting all of this energy on it?"

Early childhood trauma can make curbing anger difficult

You've learned to react with anger or impatience and therefore you can learn not to. It's more difficult for those who experienced high amounts of early childhood trauma, which can program a short fuse for your fight/flight response. Much of the trick to self-soothing is to learn to distract your mind at the earliest possible red flag of impending anger/impatience/time urgency. Ironically, you'll need to be patient to continue looking for techniques that calm you. Be persistent in using them. The more you do the sooner and better they'll soothe you.

So what else can a hothead do?

There are three main approaches to dealing with anger.

- Assertively and appropriately express it to the person with whom you're angry.
- Suppress it (but this can adversely affect your health).
- Calm it.

When you're stuck in traffic, for example:

Assertively express yourself: Communicate your needs to the appropriate people at the appropriate time in a way that does not infringe upon their needs and rights. If you cannot get what you want, then negotiate and compromise.

In traffic, with whom are you going to communicate? Other drivers? If so, be nice. No one wants to be stuck for two hours in traffic any more than you do. The overcrowding is no more their fault than it is yours. Negotiate merging into traffic. Smile, even laugh if you can.

Calm yourself with realistic expectations: Hotheads are known to have unrealistic expectations of others and of themselves. When your expectations are not met, anger is the most likely reaction.

If you're exploding in traffic, what are you expecting? Traffic to flow smoothly for some miraculous reason? Get real! ♫ Accept what is. Repeat after me, "Traffic during rush-hour is bumper to bumper and I can cope with that." Or be consciously angry and repeat,

 *"I choose to send cortisol coursing through my system."*

What are your options with this fact of life? Manage your schedule to avoid the heaviest traffic times. If you can't, accept the reality and peacefully listen to your favorite radio station, educational tapes, your favorite music, or talk about pleasant things with your passengers— anything but focus on the horribleness of the traffic.

Let positive goals guide you: By keeping a positive goal on your conscious mind, you can better calm your frustration. Let's say your positive goal in heavy traffic is to keep your stress low while creeping along. Each time your blood starts to boil say out loud, "I'm keeping my stress low. I'm focusing on things that calm me." Then do just that. Focus on things that calm you. Deep breathe.

None of these things will change the traffic. That's beyond your control. The only thing within your control is your choice of reactions. By respecting others' rights, having realistic expectations, and having your positive goal as your guide, you can tolerate the traffic better.

Emotional reactions to stress are absolutely normal. Don't allow them to dictate unproductive reactions and to allow them to continue sending cortisol coursing through your system.

Stop and Reflect

Write down a stressor that you complain about frequently.

- Whom do you usually complain to?
- When are you most likely to complain?
- Why do you complain to this person?

Why do you choose to do nothing different in response to this situation?

- What are you avoiding?
- What do you gain from doing nothing?

List at least three alternative options for dealing with your stressor.

1. _____

2. _____

3. _____

CHAPTER 8

YOUR STRESS CLIFF

A metaphor for the run-away American lifestyle

IN 2000 MY HUSBAND AND I were incredibly fortunate to be able to take off an entire year to travel throughout the United States, into Western Canada and up to Alaska in a behemoth motor home. Our coach was a luxury condo-on-six-wheels. When both slide-outs of our 40' coach were extended our living quarters were about 450 square feet. We lived in the lap of luxury along with our three cats. That's right; we traveled the entire time with our three indoor/outdoor cats.

I should mention here that this was the first time that either my husband or I had ever driven something the size of a small house.

About a month into our trip, in early January 2001, we were driving east on Interstate 70 through Utah (you know the scenic through-the-mountains-interstate) heading to glorious Aspen, Colorado for nine weeks of skiing (a sure prescription for getting rid of chronic stress and burnout is to ski for nine weeks.)

This was the first time we'd ever driven our 20-ton motor home and Jeep tow vehicle in the mountains, so we were obviously amateurs.

It was a beautiful crisp and clear day. I was videotaping the stunning Utah landscape. We were oohing and ahhing over the spectacular beauty when we saw our first real mountain grade warning sign—7% grade ahead.

Here we were, in total comfort motoring along a four-lane, divided US Interstate, traveling at the posted speed limit of 70 mph—and down the grade we went.

Do you realize how steep a 7% grade is? Do you realize how much speed a 20-ton vehicle can pick up over an especially long 7% grade? Well, hold on to your hats because this was one scary ride!

At first the descent was exciting. We were in a state-of-the-art vehicle with air suspension that made the coach float down the highway. Jake-brakes, air-brakes, power steering and brand new tires all contributed to a secure feeling. My husband, Bob, expertly switched back and forth between lanes as we gained speed down the serpentine roadway. We were still oohing and ahhing over the landscape around us.

But then Bob got frighteningly quiet. He stopped narrating for the video-cam. His face looked entirely too grim, in fact his eyes bugged out disturbingly. I became seriously nervous when our three cats deserted us and went into hiding. (You know how they say that animals sense when something catastrophic is about to happen?)

It didn't take long before we realized that our speed was picking up entirely too fast. The speedometer topped out at 85 mph and the needle was buried far beyond that. We had no idea how fast we were going but trust me, it was way too fast and was rapidly approaching out-of-control. The brakes were of little use. We had become a 20-ton runaway condo-on-six-wheels careening like a cumbersome giant down a steep and very long grade with the distinct possibility that we could fly over the cliff down into the abyss below.

Now don't get me wrong, I love adventure. I was a Peace Corps volunteer in Colombia, South America for two and a half years back in the early 70's. I have been on my share of out-of-control bus rides flying down the Andes Mountains. That was exciting! But there's a difference between being an invincible 22-year-old and a more cautious 50-year-old who wants to continue living.

What started out as an exciting trip down Interstate 70 was fast becoming life-threatening. I wouldn't even allow myself to think about encountering other vehicles on the road in front of us. (Thank goodness there were none.)

The brakes were smoking. The smell was getting worse and was permeating the coach. I can only imagine we must have looked like one of those old WWII movies where you see the smoke trailing from a damaged airplane as it plummets toward the ground.

Because we had already surpassed the speed at which the Jake-brake would slow us down, my husband had only three options for our survival:

- Keep tapping on the brakes to try to minimize further acceleration;
- Continue deftly using the two interstate lanes and their shoulders to straighten out the downhill curves, which kept the coach from leaning too much but also increased our speed; or
- Our best option: find and use a truck run-away lane to slow us down.

There were no runaway lanes so he couldn't pull off. We had to continue to white-knuckle our way down the mountain.

Finally, after what seemed like an eternity of hurtling down the mountain, the road started to slowly level off as evidenced by the coach's speedometer starting to register again; 85 mph, 80 mph assuring us we were slowing down and were going to be safe.

What did we learn from this experience?

- Eighteen wheels on the pavement are important for braking. Our motor home had only six, not anywhere near enough to slow down quickly.
- When your vehicle weighs in at 20-tons you enter mountain grades at about 35 mph, not 70!
- To slow down sufficiently before it's too late you must start tapping on the brakes much sooner!

These lessons can be translated for you to help you avoid flying over your *Stress Cliff*:

- Keep your feet (tires) on the ground by becoming more conscious. The number one way to do this is to increase your awareness of what is stressing you so you can problem-solve to reduce it. Become conscious of what you're doing to yourself. Once you have a greater understanding of the damage you're doing to yourself then I hope you'll take responsibility to do whatever it takes to lower your stress.
- ♫ Slow down you move too fast ♫: When you're already speeding through your life and you take on additional responsibilities that

increase your load and your speed, you need to slow down more often to limit the damage you do to yourself. You need to commit to several *Stress Breaks* a day.

- Tap on your brakes sooner! Don't wait until you show signs of increased physical problems, anxiety or depression before you slow down and schedule more *Stress Breaks* into your life. It could prove to be too late for some.

- Learn from your experience: If you choose not to learn and change your behavior; if you choose to keep doing the same stressful things over and over, say to yourself,

 *"I choose to send cortisol coursing through my system."*

This motor home experience is a metaphor for the run-away American lifestyle that finds too many Americans who:

- Race from here to there and back again. ♫
- Multi-task their way through each day. ♫
- Are impatient with others who are slower, finishing their thoughts for them. ♫
- Feel like tossing their computer out the window many days. ♫
- Are aggravated by many coworkers and/or family members. ♫
- Lose their cool over the ubiquitous voice mail choices that most organizations have. ♫
- Don't get enough rest. ♫
- Are accumulating multiple physical and emotional stress-related problems. ♫

Brake before going over your *Stress Cliff*

You wouldn't consider driving off a cliff in your car, would you? Yet this is what stress pushes you to do every day, physically and emotionally speaking. By creating a balance between your activity and rest you can protect yourself from this damage.

The physical fight/flight response speeds up your body and puts a momentary strain on it. If you were able to recover frequently enough from these events it would present no problem. However, since most live in a world of near-constant stress, you're probably overtaxed and under-rested.

The scary part is that this near-nonstop lifestyle has become the norm so that you may not even notice it. Over time, this underlying tension affects your thinking, emotions and behavior. Your ability to think can deteriorate, you make more mistakes and have more accidents, you may become depressed or hostile toward others, which can trigger hostility from them.

To pull back from your *Stress Cliff* channel your fight/flight energy in positive ways. There are predominantly four ways, not all positive, to channel this energy.

- Problem-solve your stressors: This is the most important skill since it reaches and hopefully resolves the underlying reasons you are stressed.
- Release the energy through physical exercise.
- Relax the energy through meditation, yoga, etc.
- Dull the fight/flight energy through too much drinking, drugs, TV, sleep, etc. I'm certainly not going to recommend you do more of this.

Remember, the trick is to create a balance between activity and rest.

Your rest patterns greatly influence the consequences of your stress. Intersperse your day with rest that may be a few seconds of deep breathing to 20 minutes of yoga or lose yourself in your favorite hobby. The more stressed and s-t-r-e-t-c-h-e-d t-o-o t-h-i-n you are, the more *Stress Breaks* you'll need to include.

Note: from now on I'll refer to all three vulnerable groups as chronic stress since anger/hostility/impatience and the runaway American lifestyle go on month-after-month, as well.

CHAPTER 9

STRESS BREAKS HELP TO PROTECT YOU

IF YOU'RE EXPERIENCING CHRONIC STRESS and therefore are susceptible to its physical and emotional consequences, you'll need to channel your fight/flight energy to protect yourself.

Think about the logic of this. It's the over-triggering of the fight/flight response without the literal fighting or fleeing physical activity that puts us in danger of developing symptoms of too much stress. So take your stress energy and do something productive with it to keep it from turning on you and harming you.

 Even if you have never suffered from chronic stress, seek an on-going balance between activity and rest. Make a commitment to doing regular *Stress Breaks* to get into and stay in great *Stress Shape* for the day when you do experience chronic stress.

Make a new pledge to yourself to let your body win:

   *"I choose to balance
the cortisol in my body."*

Stress Breaks allow your physical body, emotions and mind to return to their desired equilibrium—or at least get closer to it. In other words, the relaxation response needs to be activated after the fight/flight occurs. This can be difficult in today's runaway lifestyle when your fight/flight is triggered so frequently throughout the day leaving little chance of catching up.

When do you need to slow down?

Red flags of over-stress are very personal and it's wise to become aware of your own. If you're not familiar with them ask a trusted person what they see you doing when you're over-stressed. (Try not to snap at them if they tell you something you don't want to hear ♫.)

Then, let your symptoms motivate you to lower your stress. Become increasingly aware of how often you display the symptoms from the Symptoms Assessment from Chapter 4. Any increase in a warning sign will hopefully motivate you to use *Stress Breaks* more frequently.

Let your body win!

Remember, my main point is to let your body win by pulling yourself back from your *Stress Cliff*. You can avoid many common illnesses like colds and flues as well as put off the day of reckoning when more serious illnesses like diabetes and heart disease catch up with you. Using multiple, daily *Stress Breaks* creates more and healthier energy to do the very things that you're racing around doing putting you into better *Stress Shape* to deal with the craziness of your lifestyle.

Take multiple rests throughout your day. Naps, meditation, yoga, deep breathing can all help bring your stress response back into balance. Regularly, throughout each day, consciously bring your body back into a physical balance.

In the following two chapters you'll find a variety of *Stress Breaks* that either release your fight/flight energy or relax it. Also include anything you can think of that gives you a healthy break away from your stress. You'll notice that some of the *Stress Breaks* take 20 to 30 minutes or longer while others just require seconds. Choose the ones that you are most likely to make a habit of using. Keep in mind that if you only take *Stress Breaks* infrequently they will do little good. You must practice on a very regular basis.

Let's look at how to release your fight/flight energy first.

CHAPTER 10

RELEASE YOUR FIGHT/FLIGHT ENERGY

*"I choose to balance
the cortisol in my body."*

IT HELPS TO THINK LIKE OUR DISTANT ANCESTORS in your attempts to create more physical/emotional balance through *Stress Breaks*. Consider how physically active they were versus how sedentary we are. They took their fight/flight energy and literally used it up. We slam on the breaks of ours so as not to punch somebody out or run away from them.

How are you willing to channel the stress energy that is floating around your body because it has been denied its opportunity to fight or flee? What follows are suggestions for *Stress Breaks* you can choose from to get yourself into *Stress Shape* by pulling yourself back from your *Stress Cliff*.

Stress Break #1: REGULAR physical exercise

I would be remiss if I didn't start with this Stress Break. If we were to lead lives that were as physically active as our ancestors', chances are we would have far fewer modern diseases.

Again, let's consider the physiology of the fight/flight response. Each time your stress response is triggered your body goes through a myriad of biochemical reactions. Among these are the activation of neurotransmitters, the release of many different hormones, and metabolism of certain nutrients to speed up some physical functions (such as your cardiovascular system) and to slow down others in response to stress (such as your gastrointestinal system). All these changes are intended to help you fight better or run faster.

Regular physical exercise helps to remove the harmful effects of the fight/flight by simulating actual fighting or fleeing. Regular exercise allows your body to return to homeostasis faster and reduces the negative physical consequences of stress.

"Inactivity should be considered a disease state."
—Unknown

Anyone who's unaware of the benefits of *regular* physical exercise on mental and physical health must have been living under a rock for the past decades. If you know the importance of it and still don't exercise, then you're probably living in denial.

Research has shown over and over again that exercise diminishes the ravages of stress, decreases a variety of diseases and increases longevity. Exercise that prevents disease and builds muscles also helps you manage your stress better. It's one of the two most powerful health enhancing practices you can do; the other is deep relaxation.

It drives me nuts when people complain about being overweight, having aches and pains, not to mention illness and disease, yet don't find the wherewithal to do what they need to do to protect their health! Remaining sedentary is another way of saying you choose to put your health at risk and

 **"... I choose to send cortisol coursing through my system."**

There are countless reasons why exercise is so healthy for you. *Regular* exercise:

- Channels the fight/flight energy you generate daily, thereby keeping cortisol and other stress hormones from wearing you down physically. This is a major reason to exercise!

- *Regular* exercise decreases insulin resistance, according to neurologist Douglas Newland, M.D.

- Hiking, biking, swimming, etc. increase your brain's production of those feel-good endorphins you've heard about. Endorphins are thought to provide some pain relief and to promote a sense of euphoria. (Don't get addicted to it, though.)

- Stretching and yoga diminish muscle tension giving you more energy, calming you and helping you think more clearly. Muscles contract during your fight/flight response. Exercising releases your muscles' stored energy allowing them to return to a balanced—and less stressed—state, so you'll have fewer tension headaches, arthritis and back pain.

- Physical fitness increases your sense of self-control, which increases your self-confidence in other areas of your life and minimizes symptoms of mild depression and anxiety. Anything that increases healthy self-control diminishes stress.

- You'll sleep better, too, (presuming you don't exercise to exhaustion—or vigorously too close to bedtime) allowing you to perform at higher levels during your awake hours. Since *regular* exercise keeps your cortisol levels at a more normal level, and because insomnia is often caused by too high a cortisol level at night, it makes sense to exercise more versus take sleeping pills.

- Exercise also strengthens your physical systems so you're in better shape to fight possible future illness and disease plus you'll be able to recover more quickly from them.

- Anger management: Remember that research has pointed to the role that anger and hostility play in cardiovascular disease. Exercise is a socially-acceptable way to vent this caustic emotion.

- Increase in self-confidence: You get a sense of accomplishment through *regular* exercise, not to mention the boost to self-esteem when you start to look better.

- Increase in self-esteem and self-control: *Regularly* engaging in such a healthy practice is evidence that you value yourself, which leads to greater self-esteem. Seeing the positive results in your body from *regular* exercise also demonstrates to you that you do have control over yourself.

- It's much better to exercise away your stress than to reach for another drink or legal or illegal drugs.

- Exercise is one of the best treatments for depression and anxiety.

- Etc., etc., etc. There's simply not much in this world that's healthier for you (besides love and that good stuff).

You don't have to start running marathons to benefit from exercise. According to the Mayo Clinic, virtually any form of exercise can decrease the production of stress hormones and channel your fight/flight energy in healthy ways.

You can start small. If you know that you don't get enough exercise, get more. If you now get winded from walking two blocks, walk two blocks until you don't get winded then increase to three, then four, etc.

Which exercise most appeals to you? Walking? Sports? (Please don't say channel-surfing.) It makes no difference as long as it's regular and safe for you, your abilities and age.

To increase the likelihood that you'll start to exercise, make your goal of getting more fit a step in achieving a larger life goal, such as living to see your grandchildren born and grow! When you see how exercise can help you reach a bigger goal it gives it more meaning and therefore you're more likely to follow through. Make it happen!

Exercise for a better mental state

The hothead's face turns red; that vein in her temple throbs; she's about to blow. She might blow herself right into a heart attack! For her heart and overall physical health and the health of her relationships, she'd be wise to exercise out her angry energy.

The same goes for those who suffer from depression or anxiety. Exercise helps curb these mental states. But if getting out of bed feels overwhelming, exercising can seem impossible. The degree of mood improvement with regular exercise, though, is so significant that many believe it's more effective than counseling and anti-depressants.

Small amounts of exercise are better than none and can prevent a relapse after treatment for these conditions. Kristin Vickers-Douglas, Ph.D., a Mayo Clinic psychologist, says, "Small bouts of exercise may be a great way to a get started if it's initially too difficult to do more." If ten minutes is all you'll do, then do ten minutes.

It's not completely understood why exercise decreases mood disorder symptoms. It's probably due to cortisol reduction and increased endorphins and body temperature, which may have calming effects.

Plus, exercise is a great substitute for the obsessive thinking that drives all of these difficult emotions. Wherever your thoughts are going that's where you are going; anxious thoughts lead you to anxiety. By exercising you burn up your fight/flight energy in a positive way, distracting you from obsessive thinking about how miserable you are.

To get motivated to exercise:

- First, talk with your physician and/or mental health professional for advice and support.
- Next, figure out what you enjoy doing. If you hate exercise participate in a sport that you enjoy. You'll be more likely to stick with it.
- Set realistic goals. Create a long-term goal with shorter-term intermediate steps. If your ultimate goal is to walk daily for 30 minutes, start with 5 to 10 minutes every day for the first month, the next month walk for 15 to 20 minutes, and so on. Avoid unreasonable goals that you're unlikely to achieve. This makes you feel worse about yourself, aggravating your symptoms.
- Accept that if you fall off the wagon, and most of us do, you just have to start again.
- Stop thinking that you should exercise; that's a weight (no pun intended) you don't need. Instead, convince yourself of the benefits.
- Isolation is common among those who are depressed and anxious, worsening symptoms, so consider exercising with others. Social contact decreases your symptoms and helps you meet your exercise goal.

Take the advice of Dr. Mary Ann Chapman, "The key to breaking a bad habit (doing nothing) and adopting a good one (exercising) is making changes in your daily life that minimize the influence of the now and remind you of the later." In other words:

- Minimize the immediate reward of doing nothing (relief from not exercising).
- Make the long-term negative consequences of not exercising (continued depression/anxiety/anger) seem more immediate.

So instead of excuse after excuse to avoid exercise, remind yourself how tired you are of being emotionally stuck and exhausted.

Yoga is one of the best ways to exercise

Yoga, part of the Hindu religion whose ultimate goal is reaching complete mind/body peacefulness, provides great stress reduction benefits; even if you don't practice the philosophy side of it.

Yoga ranks right at the top of good things you can do for yourself to reduce the harmful effects of stress. It's not a cure-all, but when combined with other healthy practices it can facilitate better health. It's a wonderful way to get the benefits of:

- Relaxation and stress reduction: yoga's breathing is instant stress reduction since it's the opposite of the fight/flight shallow breathing.

- Chronic illness management: yoga is known to help asthma, depression, back pain, carpal tunnel syndrome, multiple sclerosis, heart disease, high blood pressure, osteoarthritis, and pretty much anything that afflicts humanity.

- Greater mental focus.

- Mindfulness (being more tuned into your body so you can know when it's trying to send you a message that you need to slow down ♫ or fix something).

- Increased flexibility and balance: yoga instructors have you move only as much as is comfortable for you. Gradually you'll find yourself stretching more and more—far beyond where you started. You'll develop greater range of motion, which helps to protect you from injury in other activities.

These days there are many yoga classes in virtually every community. Consider having a private session with an instructor you like so she can prescribe certain exercises for you personally.

I did this after my parents passed away when my body was left in a state of chronic stress. As I mentioned earlier, I was so stressed (even though I'd continued with my Yoga and other *Stress Breaks* throughout their illnesses) it felt like I could break a bone just sitting around. My friend and Yoga teacher, Debbie, gave me a private session. I told her where I held my stress, how many minutes worth of exercise I was willing to do daily (10–12 minutes) and she watched me do certain movements. She then prescribed exercises tailored to meet my specific needs.

These were a life-saver for me. Over the six months after my parents died I could feel a little bit of muscle tension leave my body every day that I did my Yoga exercises. No other exercise was able to remove the muscle tension from my body like Yoga did. It's now over 10 years since my parents passed away and I still do these same exercises two to three times a week.

Yoga's risks

Even though Yoga is considered to be very safe if you're generally healthy, some positions can put strain on your lower back and joints. Consult with your doctor first if you have any joint, back or neck problems. Of course, if you're pregnant, consult with your doctor first.

Stress Break #2: Tense/relax muscles

Part of the fight/flight response is muscle tension. The more stressed you are the more muscle tension you experience. If you remain stressed too long your muscles stay tensed, exhausting you. Here's a great exercise that requires absolutely no will power or drastic change, such as regular exercise can. This exercise physically channels your stress energy.

- Starting with your head and moving down through your entire body, tighten every single muscle group (from your eyes and jaw to the tips of your fingers and toes) for ten to fifteen seconds. Don't tense to the point of hurting yourself but to the point that you shake a bit. Then relax completely and notice the difference in the feeling between tension and relaxation.
- Repeat the tense/relax cycle two to three times daily.
- When finished, if any muscles still feel tight, go back and tense/relax them a time or two more.

To sleep better: If you have trouble sleeping at night because you're physically hyper, do the tense/relax exercise nightly before going to sleep. Unless you're drinking 22 cups of coffee it should help you sleep better.

To avoid choking someone: To avoid the instinct of flying across the table and choking your nemesis or running away from him, repetitively tense and relax your muscles (just the ones that are hidden from view, of course).

This creates greater physical balance therefore mental balance allowing you to think more clearly about how to handle him.

Stress Break #3: Laugh your way to a healthy life

An excellent way to reduce stress, therefore cortisol, is to find humor in taxing situations. This isn't always possible or appropriate but usually it is. Interpreting life with a sense of humor is not the same as telling jokes. It's looking for, finding, using and appreciating life's humor to serve as your shock absorbers to stress.

"If you can find humor in something you can survive it," said Bill Cosby. It helps neutralize emotions to make coping easier. How true I have found this to be!

During my parents end-of-life-illnesses we relied on humor to soften the blow of the incredible stress of having both of them failing at the same time. I've always referred to this time in our lives as a very good, bad time. Humor is what put the good into it.

One of many examples I still fondly remember was when my father was in the ICU for the first time. He couldn't talk because he was on a ventilator but was trying so hard to communicate something to my mother and me. With no teeth in his mouth and a tube down his throat we had absolutely no idea what he was trying to say.

For 30 minutes we guessed. The communication aides the nurses gave us didn't help. After each one of our guesses my father would shake his head in frustration. Finally, my mother said to my father, "Are you asking why you can't talk?" With great relief he nodded elatedly. We all burst out laughing uncontrollably. We climbed this mountain together and our reward, as it was all our lives, was a good laugh. The positive feelings from this stayed with us long after the situation had passed.

Laughter elevates your mood in difficult situations and miraculously melts away your anger and anxiety. Like my high-school boyfriend who, at the age of 17, was fighting mad one night and threw a common middle finger nonverbal at the person he was angry with. Then suddenly he was reminded that his middle finger hand been blown off in a chemistry experiment accident. He burst out laughing at the absurdity of it all, which allowed him to walk away from the building altercation. Finding what is ridiculous in some of your own reactions and interpretations creates greater objectivity about yourself and gives you a much better perspective in your more challenging situations.

Looking for and finding the humor in tense situations can diminish the immensity of the problem as well as open your mind to previously unseen options. Humorous interpretations flex your perception muscles expanding your mind's ability to search for options. This is one of humor's greatest benefits; humorous thinking is basically the same as creative thinking. When you're unable to resolve a stressor, find the humor in it and you'll be closer to finding a creative solution.

Humor helps you deal better with almost any situation because:

- It facilitates mental flexibility and increases creativity by lightening negative emotions allowing you to think through problems instead of only emotionally muddling through them.
- Team building is facilitated by shared humor. (Not the divisive type like sarcasm or humor aimed at belittling anyone or any group, of course.)
- "The shortest distance between two people is humor," said the famed comedic pianist, Victor Borge. Humor improves most communication, especially when it's potentially confrontational.
- It's just fun.

Health benefits of laughter

Psychoneuroimmunology research is expanding dramatically. This research looks for relationships between emotional experiences and your immune system's response to them as directed by your neurological system. Here's a sampling of what researchers are finding:

- Physically and mentally laughter is the opposite of stress. It lowers blood pressure, increases blood circulation, reduces muscle tension and pain, and boosts your immune system.
- Seeing humor diminishes depression, which is very important because depressed people are more prone to illnesses like high blood pressure, heart attacks, and a weakened immune system.
- Laughter can reduce aches and pains by taking your mind off them.

- Laughter increases circulation and improves the delivery of oxygen and nutrients to the body.
- Strong laughter is good for competitive athletes, as well. Because breathing capacity determines stamina, athletes who experience hearty laughter before an event increase their relaxation level which can enhance their performance.
- Humor lowers blood pressure. Those who laugh often and vigorously have a lower standing blood pressure than the average person. This causes their breathing to become deeper sending oxygen-enriched blood throughout the body.
- Laughter aides the immune system in doing its job properly warding off respiratory problems like an aerobic workout does for your lungs. When you have a good belly laugh you expel more air resulting in a cleansing effect similar to that of deep breathing.
- Laughter reduces epinephrine and cortisol, which are associated with stress.
- Laughter helps control pain by increasing endorphins and allowing the body to relax.
- Laughter facilitates muscle relaxation since it requires muscle tensing which is followed by greater muscle relaxation than before the laughter.

Researchers, such as Michael Miller, University of Maryland School of Medicine, have studied humor's effect on your health. Knowing that blood vessels constrict when you're stressed making you more vulnerable to circulation problems, he wondered if laughter could loosen them. His study showed that blood flow decreased about 35% after experiencing stress but increased 22% after laughter, an improvement equal to about a 15-minute workout. Wouldn't you love your physician to prescribe 15 minutes of laughter every day? The good news is that you can prescribe this to yourself!

Other research has shown that stress hormones like cortisol and epinephrine cause circulation changes. It stands to reason that laughter may cause the release of pleasure producing endorphins that may counteract stress hormones and increase blood flow.

Lee Berk is an associate professor of health promotion and education at Loma Linda University, where he studies laughter. He said, "Laughter is not dissimilar to exercise. It's not going to cure stage-three cancer but in terms of prevention it does make sense."

Dr. Berk, along with fellow researcher Dr. Stanley Tan, has found through controlled studies that laughter, "stimulates the immune system [counteracting] the immunosuppressive effects of stress" by lowering cortisol thereby protecting your immune system.

Humor may also be good for your career. A Robert Half International survey found 84% of top corporate officers thought employees with a sense of humor do better at work than those with little or no sense of humor.

Here are examples from workshop participants where humor reduced their stress:

- The most gorgeous redhead I'd ever met told me she used to get defensive when meeting many men who'd invariably say in a suggestive voice, "Ooh, a redhead!" She'd angrily react with a death-grip hand shake. She knew this didn't serve her well. She knew that when you react defensively to anything you appear powerless. Knowing that humor is an opposite of defensiveness, she searched for a humorous (therefore less defensive) way to deal with such remarks. She settled on, "Ooh, a blackhead!"and found the men always got it. She appeared non-defensive, which enhanced her professional image.

- To lighten her load over something beyond her control, a woman who'd had a mastectomy said she jokingly demanded her mammograms at half-price.

- Child rearing can frazzle any parent. My father had a wonderful sense of humor and used it to soften a "no". For instance, during the long, cold Minnesota winters I'd whine that other kids got rides to school but I had to walk, risking life and limb. He seemed to listen seriously then responded, "Well, when you get tired of walking— run!" I'd roll my eyes and walk out the door chuckling.

- Cheer up your office with visual humor like the desk sign that reads, "If you'll just state your business and go away quietly no one will get hurt." Or just for fun, head your next memo with, "To whom this may irritate."

Nourish your sense of humor by looking for it:

Seeing humor in otherwise stressful events simply makes life more enjoyable. In order to find the humor however you've got to look for it.

- Do things differently and become more aware of life around you. Vary your routines. Take a different route to work. Change your lunch habit. Look for and find five things that make you smile. Keep looking and you'll keep finding things that tickle you.

- Keep a humor file. Add bits like this odd newspaper headline, "Good Samaritans may get stun guns." That's funny! Cheer yourself up by reading what's in your file when you need a *Stress Break*.

- Approach your day with a sense of playfulness. Play with kids and pets.

- Exaggerate: When having a bad day, exaggerate it and have a really bad day. Complain endlessly about how rotten everything is, how uncooperative others are (not to mention how stupid and ugly).

- Accept and gently poke fun at your own imperfections. An obese woman who'd accepted her appearance in a swimsuit would saunter up to people on the beach who were seemingly talking about her and sweetly say to them, "What's the matter, haven't you ever seen a pretty girl before?" This made her feel much better than her historic defensive and hurtful response.

- Imagine your favorite comedian(s) having your silly family arguments.

The more serious (and possibly even sour) you are the more you're missing out on life and the more cortisol you allow to course through your system. If you'd increase the number of things that make you smile over the next year you will have less stress and become a more creative problem solver. Those smiles eventually lead to chuckles, which eventually will lead to outright and wonderful laughter. It's a no-lose choice because the worse case scenario is you'll have more fun—and lower your cortisol in the process.

Stop and Reflect

Laugh Your Way to a Healthy Life

Write a brief description of a stressor you are having difficulty resolving.

Rewrite it in an exaggerated way. Make mountains out of molehills. Exaggerate to the point of being silly. Humor is in the ridiculous.

What would your favorite comedian find funny about your situation?

Stress Break #4: Journal out your heart

If you haven't yet discovered the power of keeping a journal about your life's ups and downs, then you've been missing out on a very good stress reduction friend.

Eldridge Cleaver, the 1960's civil rights activist said, "If you're not part of the solution, you're part of the problem." Keeping a journal about your stressors allows you to be more a part of the solution.

Pouring your heart out into a personal journal is incredibly healthy and helpful because it:

- Allows you to let go of some of your stressful obsessing, which dumps stress hormones into your body.

- Helps you understand if your focus about a stressor is part of the problem or part of the solution. (Remember, stress is in the mind of the beholder; often what's stressing you is not the outside event you're focused on but rather your interpretation of it.)

- Encourages creative ideas to float up from the unconscious to help you relieve your stressors.

- Helps you see if you're focusing on the things that are within your control or beyond your control (the subject of my next stress reduction book.) Focusing too much on what's beyond your control may explain much of your stress. It's OK to vent about those things through journaling and talking to others. But once you've vented, focus your energy on problem-solving: what you can fix and learn to cope with what you can't.

- Lowering your stress lowers the fight/flight response, limiting the cortisol coursing through your system.

Keep a journal about your challenging stressors. Write or draw whatever pops out regarding whatever you feel like journaling about.

Journal: unload your deepest thoughts and feelings

To problem-solve on a stressor, versus just venting about it, choose a specific stressor that troubles you. Don't use, for example, my job. This is too general. Choose a job stressor such as handling angry customers. Since questions engage your brain to search for answers, write your stressor in question form, e.g. how can I better handle angry customers?

Next, pour your heart into your journal about this challenge knowing that no one else will read it. Let whatever wants to come out come. Don't force any thoughts. Shoot for stream of consciousness journaling whether you write or draw. Stream of consciousness means:

- Let out whatever wants to come out.
- Let go of pre-determining what you'll journal.
- Let go of editing; don't worry about spelling, grammar, etc. Don't fuss about how bad you are at drawing, either.
- Let go of judging; just let it come.

Follow these steps to increase the value of your journaling experience:

- Keep your regularly used journal, whether an appealing and decorative one or a spiral notebook, handy. Keep as many journals as you like. You could keep one for work, one for home, etc.
- Open your mind to drawing instead of writing. Have colored pencils or crayons and draw—even stick-figure drawings, whatever pops into your mind. Because drawing is more symbolic you may get deeper insights from it than from writing.
- You can either start to journal with an intended focus or you can spontaneously journal about anything.
- To focus on something specific, start with a question to engage your brain in problem-solving.

- Seek uninterrupted time; your focus will be better.

- Use relaxing music and deep breathing to access more of your intuitive unconscious mind.

- Date all of your entries.

The window to your intuitive, creative, unconscious (ICU) is a quiet mind

Depending upon your goal, it's usually best to quiet your mind before you journal. This allows you much greater access to a deep level of understanding and insights that can help resolve whatever is stressing you. You're more likely to find better answers to your questions and solutions to your stressors when you quiet yourself first.

If your journaling goal is simply to get rid of distracting thinking so you can go to sleep more easily, for instance, you don't need to quiet yourself first. Just put down any and all thoughts that come to your mind.

To quiet yourself:

- Start by sitting comfortably in a room with dim lighting; take several deep breaths until you notice your body relaxing more. There's a point when your body almost sighs to indicate it's very relaxed. Once there, begin to journal.

- Start with meditation (see Chapter 11.) After 15 to 20 minutes, begin your journaling. This is when you can expect to get your best insights, even epiphanies.

- After you're quieted either from deep breathing and/or from deep relaxation, in a relaxed way just put pen or color pencil to paper and let come out whatever wants to come out.

Keep in mind that whatever insights you gain from journaling don't have to be acted upon immediately. It's very powerful, however, to let those insights into your conscious mind because the brain has an incredible way of allowing you to eventually act in your best interests based on the truths your journaling surfaces.

For example, a workshop participant, Tonya, said her journaling assignment told her she had to quit her job. But with a mortgage and two kids still in school she was stressed by this because, in her mind, she couldn't afford to quit. She told me several months later that she attended a professional meeting one day and ran into an old colleague who offered her a much better and less stressful job on the spot! She took the offer and believes that she had to release the truth about having to leave her old job before she would have been open to this new opportunity.

Over time, through journaling, you can develop greater trust in your own inner wisdom to guide you in problem-solving and decision-making.

Stop and Reflect

Develop Journaling

- Write down a stressor to journal about. It can be the same one you chose earlier as you searched for humor or something else you are struggling with.

- Make a commitment to spend time journaling about this stressor. Write down the date and time when you will begin.

- Follow some of the suggestions outlined in Stress Break 4. Good luck!

Stress Break #5: Do more that gives you pleasure, passion and/or joy!

Emotional balance is an important component of effective stress management partly because it allows you to see your stressors more objectively. Emotional imbalance also triggers your fight/flight response sending cortisol coursing through your system. Bringing pleasure, passion and/or joy to your life not only makes the difficult emotional times easier it also brings you more emotional balance, therefore less stress.

As my parents' major caregiver (along with my husband, siblings, hospitals, an assisted care facility and eventually a nursing home) during their end of life illnesses, the stress was unbelievable. I've never known so much. When I came dragging myself home from a particularly tough day, our two young kittens would bounce all over me. Laughter was a split second away. They helped me shed some of the stressful emotions, which allowed me to think more clearly about things.

Here is a quick test to see what you are presently doing to create and maintain your emotional balance:

In 30 seconds, count on your fingers the number of things you do regularly (weekly, monthly, even annually) that bring you pleasure, passion and/or joy. Do this now—30 seconds.

Why do I suggest 30 seconds? Because, if you were left scratching your head trying to think of things you do regularly, it probably means you aren't doing much of anything. This most likely makes the emotional side of all of your stress more difficult to handle.

Bring more activities into your life that will bring you pleasure, passion or joy—or all three.

- According to research from the growing field of Positive Psychology the helpful effects of doing something pleasurable like being with friends or buying something you've wanted, pale in comparison with the effects of doing something kind for another person. Can you volunteer for a favorite cause? Or do you have a neighbor who could use a helping hand?

- Identify what could bring you enjoyment. On your deathbed, what will you say you wished you would have done more of? Dance? Spend time with your family? Travel? Whatever your answer, do more of that now. Even if you can't afford to travel, for instance, start by looking at travel magazines or TV shows to begin planning or fantasizing about where you'd go.

- Over the next month, observe what makes you smile and feel good inside. Whatever triggered the smile is most likely another thing that could bring you pleasure.

- What did you used to do that brought you pleasure? Art? Perform music? A hobby? Can you begin to do that again?

- What do other people do that looks enjoyable to you? Try that. Give yourself the assignment to do one thing every week for the sheer sake of enjoyment. Go ahead! See what happens!

Life is too short to miss the good stuff. The more pleasure you have in your life the more you are protected from depression and the better you'll handle difficult emotions when they do arise. The better you handle the difficult emotions the better you'll handle the stress that is triggering them. All of this leads to greater emotional balance and allows you to be a more creative stress manager.

Stop and Reflect

Create more pleasure, passion and joy!

- If you were on your deathbed, how would you finish the statement, "I wish I had done more _____."
- List three things right now that you know make you smile or touch your heart.
- List a least two activities you enjoyed in the past that you could begin to do again.
- List at least two things you see others doing that you think you might enjoy.
- It is healthy to do at least one thing each week simply for pleasure or fun. What would you do the first week?

Stress Break # 6: Spend time with friends

In the cookies of life, friends are the chocolate chips. Friends are the sweet and special in life, plus they help reduce your stress.

Let's revisit UCLA psychologist Shelley Taylor's theory about the "tend and befriend" response. University of California scientists report that women seem to be programmed hormonally to use relationships in response to life's problems in a way that men aren't. The oxytocin women release, especially in conjunction with estrogen, is calming, possibly limiting the damage from stress hormones. (Men's testosterone floods their systems during stress, which inhibits oxytocin.) Doctor Taylor's theory supports what women have always known: friendships are healthy for us. What a treat it is to learn that they might actually minimize the damage of the stress response. Additionally, University of Pittsburgh research found that social support reduces cardiovascular reactivity to psychological challenges. There's something calming about having friends when you're stressed. They can help reduce your stress, therefore, the cortisol coursing through your system.

According to the Mayo Clinic having close friends and family on whom you can depend has extensive health benefits. Friendship allows you to connect with others, increasing your sense of belonging, purpose and self-esteem, which promotes mental wellness. Having trustworthy friends to share your life also reduces your unhealthy reactions to stressful events.

Social neuroscience, the study of how the brain referees social interactions, is adding to our understanding of how this might work.

Mirror neurons in the brain have been found to track the emotional flow and even the intentions of the person we're with. Then our own brains duplicate this perceived state by stimulating the same brain areas activated in the other person. It seems that this facilitates interpersonal synchronization of physiological changes, too.

Mirror neurons might explain why we tend to catch other people's emotional states. They may also explain rapport, the unconscious mirroring of another's nonverbal behaviors and vocal patterns as you interact. The more you mirror one another the more in rapport you are, therefore the more trusting and cooperative you'll be.

Harmonization of brain states, emotions and cardiovascular reactions between people have been studied in mothers and their infants, spouses arguing and people in meetings. Drs. Lisa M. Diamond and Lisa G. Aspinwall, University of Utah psychologists, have reviewed decades' worth of data and have found that emotional closeness allows the biology of one person to influence another's.

As the University of Chicago's Dr. John T. Cacioppo, director of the Center for Cognitive and Social Neuroscience, says, "In short, my hostility bumps up your blood pressure, your nurturing love lowers mine," making us each other's biological enemies or allies.

I am hugely blessed in this arena of close friendships. There are an even dozen in my personal circle of female friends. Our love and closeness also extend to everyone's husbands and children. We've been through decades of ups and downs and are closer because of it. Through everything, our love and acceptance has spanned 26 years. We're very aware of our great fortune.

Friendships like these don't just happen, they require lots of investment.

What goes around comes around; to receive unconditional love and support from others you must also give it.

You don't have time, you say, to nurture friendships? This is true only if you think it is. If you value friendship enough you'll make the time. Even during our child-raising-phases we scheduled near monthly events for just the girls and many weekend events for the families. Not everyone attended everything, but mostly we did.

It's hard to make new friends, you counter? Perhaps, but it's worth figuring out a way to find and nurture them. This circle of friends came together in the early 1980s when we were involved in common community causes. We all joined organizations out of our commitment and passion to these social causes and through them we met each other.

It took the initiative of one of the women, Stephanie, to invite the rest of us together for the first time. We had a raucous and fun time from the very beginning. She continued to get us all together time and again, until the group energy eventually took on a life of its own. And here we are 26 years later, with more wrinkles, some new husbands, and eternal gratefulness for each other.

You don't have to have a dozen close friends. One or two will do. But you need friends outside of your family for objectivity, variety and potential for growth.

Friends are better for you than watching TV!

Often, however, those in most need of friendship spend inordinate amounts of time in solo, passive pursuits. The General Social Survey (GSS) over 34 years of collecting data has found that those who are happy report being more active in social activities, including religion, and report less time watching television.

So, instead, take a risk and try these ideas to expand your support system:

- Don't wait for someone else to make the first move. Initiate get-togethers with those you think you could be friends with. It won't always pan out but when it does, it's so worth it.

- Follow your interests and meet like-minded people by joining groups that already appeal to you, like a college class or a political cause.

- Be discerning about whom to befriend. Someone who's not supportive of you causes more stress instead of reducing it.

- Accept that relationships are two-way streets. To receive unconditional love and supportive attention you must give it.

- Don't overwhelm someone with phone calls or invitations. Consider that if they're not getting back to you after a few attempts it may be their way of saying they're not interested.

- Walk your pet, join a gym and seek out opportunities to chat with others. Don't pressure anyone to be your friend, just let conversations evolve. If there's potential for friendship it'll emerge.

- Accept others' invitations to events even if you fear you won't know anyone. The worst case scenario is you become bored and leave early.

- Open yourself up to conversations. Don't put your conversational partner through a friendship test, just enjoy talking.

- Be visible in your neighborhood. Sit on the front porch, take walks, attend sponsored community activities, get to know your neighbors.

- If you know you have personality traits that historically turned off friends, work to reduce them or develop a sense of humor about them. Poke fun at your own tendency to complain or to be needy.

Close relationships, it seems, are important to your health and resiliency to illness. To protect yourself, keep your relationships in good shape. Surround yourself with people who are your biological allies and avoid or insulate yourself from those who are your enemies.

Stress Break # 7: Pursue "flow" activities

In the introduction to his wonderful book, *Finding Flow*, Mihaly Csikszentmihalyi says, " . . . we often walk through our days . . . out of touch with our emotional lives. As a result of this inattention, we find ourselves constantly bouncing between two extremes: during much of the day we live inundated by the . . . pressures of our work and obligations, and during our leisure moments, we tend to live in passive boredom."

To avoid this uninspiring lifestyle he encourages creating goals on which to focus. " . . . goals shape and determine the kind of person you become.

Without them it's difficult to develop a coherent self." He says to engage in activities that require a high degree of skill and commitment. Instead of watching television, perfect a hobby, transform a routine task with a new goal, "learn the joy of complete engagement" by making desirable and undesirable tasks into flow activities by:

- Defining your goal.
- Creating a sense of control.
- Getting relevant feedback on how you're doing.
- Stretching your skills to reach your goal.
- Having uninterrupted focus.
- Appreciating what you're doing but it isn't necessary.

For example, for me, skiing is a flow activity.

- My goal: enjoy the challenge while getting safely to the bottom of the hill.
- I mostly ski within my limits to give me control.
- My feedback: not falling too frequently and reaching the bottom in one piece.
- Believe me, I'm stretching my skills to ski at all, let alone at the speed at which I ski!
- The time is uninterrupted; I'm completely focused.
- I love the challenge, the beautiful surroundings, and the wind rushing by my cold ears!

Flow can come from work involvements!

It's typical of Americans to think that if they just didn't have to work they could add plenty of happiness (flow) to their lives. But, take it from me, after nine months of our year-long sabbatical my husband and I were both ready to return to a normal life. A Canadian RV park manager said it perfectly, "You can only play so long."

Too many people dread work and live for their weekends. Bill Cosby did a great stand-up routine poking fun at those who drag themselves through their work-week anxiously awaiting their weekends just so they can stuff themselves with every bad habit, food and drink possible. Then they haul themselves back to work on Mondays to suffer through yet another work week.

Besides, spending your leisure time passively without goals and without stretching your skills not only doesn't produce flow it actually fuels stressful thinking.

Interestingly, Csikszentmihalyi found that the majority of your peak experiences are from work, which may surprise you. However, some jobs don't offer much opportunity for flow because:

- The work is meaningless.
- It provides no variety or challenge.
- It's too stressful, especially when there are many interpersonal problems.

To create more flow on the job your challenge is to put more meaning into your work. Don't wait for your boss to do it for you. Figure it out yourself:

- Add value to any task by knowing how it impacts the entire operation. For example, filing paperwork seems meaningless unless you understand that it facilitates your coworkers' quick access to information so they can improve customer service.
- Accept that the way things are being done is not necessarily the only way. Look for new and better ways to improve the outcome.
- Enhance your skills in each challenge. For example, a toll booth worker decided to make her job more interesting and challenging by setting a goal to get 25% of her customers to smile at her as they tossed their money at her, thereby improving her customer service skills. After she achieved that, she increased her goal to 50%. When this no longer motivated her she'd look for other ways to improve.

Turn mundane chores into flow activities

An example of this might be to make a goal to organize your errands from the furthest away to the closest (or vice versa) to save time and gas money.

- Your new goal requires you to sit and think of your route before heading out, which increases your control over the tasks.
- Your feedback is whether or not you have to back track for some task

you missed. If there's no backtracking then you've accomplished your goal.

- Make your goal require that you stretch your skills such as requiring you to plan your route and think of anything you have to take with you before you leave rather than the haphazard and spontaneous approach you normally take.

- Focus completely on your planning to accomplish your goal.

- Take pride in your accomplished goal, increased efficiency, and mileage and money conserved.

Mundane chores can add to a boring life that generates very little motivation. You can increase your control, therefore lower your stress, by turning daily activities into flow activities.

Stop and Reflect

Turn your mundane responsibilities into flow activities.

- What project you are working on now where you would like to create more flow?

- Write a goal to improve the outcome of this project.

- How can your new goal create greater control for you?

- How will you measure success?

- How does your new goal require stretching your skills?

- How will working toward it improve your focus on your project?

Flow activities help decrease negative thinking and feeling

When you're not actively focusing on something do your thoughts easily drift to what's wrong in your life? This is very common and it causes great stress. Wherever your thoughts are going, that's where you are going. Thinking about what's wrong in your life leads you to miss what is going well.

Csikszentmihalyi says that when your attention isn't focused on goals your mind wanders and settles on the negative. This leads to distracting yourself through passive leisure activities like TV, drugs, etc.

Operating in flow prohibits distracting thoughts and negative feelings because your attention is so focused on accomplishing something. Minor aches and pains also drift to the background of your awareness.

To balance your moods, strive for flow through your clearly defined goals that stretch your skills to overcome a challenge that's almost manageable—not too easy nor difficult. You'll be motivated by and focused on the activity which becomes effortless, even when the goal is difficult to achieve. You can lose track of time.

To be in flow, remember that you need valid and immediate feedback on how well you're doing. So, in dealing with an upset customer your feedback is how quickly (or not!) he calms down.

Take charge of your moods and thoughts by focusing on the task at hand, whether pleasant or unpleasant, leisure or professional. Set and achieve goals that challenge your skills and notice your unpleasant moods start to fade.

Balance between being in the current moment and pursuit of goals

Balance: a state of equilibrium, equal distribution of weight, amount, etc. Seeking balance in your life is a cornerstone of stress management; such as don't under- or over-exercise, if you're too passive you'd be wise to become more assertive, etc.

Following Csikszentmihalyi's advice can create a life of greater meaning and happiness and less ruminating on the negative.

But some people take this to the extreme, putting far too much energy into pursuing goals leading to a state of imbalance. They continually focus on the future while missing much of today, like the hard-driving successful person who approaches a beautiful sunset without even noticing it. Being goal-oriented is great, but not to the exclusion of the here and now.

Others would say focusing on future goals is largely a waste of time because, as Buddhists believe, one's reality is in the present moment; the here and now. To practitioners, focusing on the future means missing reality. Besides, working so tirelessly on goal attainment often doesn't bring you the satisfaction you'd hoped for anyway. Another benefit of living in the moment is that it facilitates mental and emotional balance because it means giving up your worries about the future and your regrets about the past.

But focusing exclusively on the here and now may not prepare you for the future. The reality of living in our economic society, for example, requires knowing where your next paycheck is coming from to pay bills and that requires at least some level of planning for the future.

This is where balance comes in. Over-focusing on tomorrow means missing today; ask parents who over-focused on careers and missed out on their kids growing up.

Over-focusing on today may find someone in love with the spontaneous but forgetting important work deadlines or other commitments.

The trick is to seek balance. The more an imbalance pushes down one side of the scale the more you need to rectify it by doing something quite different to create a better equilibrium.

For example, you high-speeders racing into the future might want to balance your goal-focused tendencies by increasing your mindfulness of things you do daily, like playing with your kids and focusing your attention on their touch, adorability, and the good feelings inside you when you interact in a loving way with them. Regular meditation would be great for you and would allow you to be more aware of the present.

Or if you tend to mostly live in the moment, scraping together your rent money, prepare a budget and figure out where your necessary income will come from. Set goals of how to adjust your income and expenses.

Balancing how much you focus on the present and the future allows you to enjoy the opportunities of the moment as well as plan for and secure your future.

Stress Break # 8: Immerse yourself in a volunteer effort or a hobby that you love

Helping others is an effective way to fight stress and depression

In August 2004, after Hurricane Charley ravaged Southwest Florida there was a Michigan couple in their 70s who plotted visits to hurricane victims' homes using local maps as they negotiated southwest Florida's increasingly frustrating traffic. There were counselors from Colorado, Mississippi, Minnesota, Illinois, and a widow from Arkansas who had been volunteering around the country for over 40 years. They interacted with emergency workers and survivors of the hurricane to lend an ear and to be available for those in distress. There were volunteers who joyfully fed thousands in need of a hot meal while others helped clear people's property of downed trees and debris. Why do they do this work?

Some would say it's American to respond to people in need. And they're right. It's also human nature. Everywhere I've ever traveled and lived, neighbors help neighbors. Most automatically reach out to those in need. What's different in this country versus poorer countries is that we also have a government response that puts muscle, speed and money behind these efforts.

Others would say that reaching out to those in need is hard-wired into our brains to increase human survival. That's probably true, too. The survival of a society increases the survival of the individual and vice versa.

There must be something more, though, to helping others. There must be something to connecting with others in a very basic human and positive way.

Could volunteering be a natural anti-depressant? Some believe it's impossible to feel depressed when you help another person. I don't know about impossible but I do believe helping others is a great way to reduce depression and stress, therefore cortisol. It takes your mind away from focusing on what's wrong and refocuses it by connecting with others. It stimulates the part of the brain that experiences positive emotions.

As a temporary local volunteer with the Red Cross after the hurricane, the looks of gratitude I saw on the faces of people receiving assistance after the hurricane and the looks of satisfaction on the faces of the volunteers giving it touched my heart time and time again.

The Institute of Volunteering Research found that for older people, voluntary work can help maintain a sense of purpose and self-respect, increase life satisfaction, lessen social isolation, and have beneficial effects on physical and mental health. In other words, it feels good to help someone. The same benefits are there for everyone.

In the weeks and months of on-going chronic stress from whatever its source, reach out and help someone. Volunteer with a cause you believe in whether it's religious or community based. It helps you feel better, to be less stressed and depressed, and commits you to something bigger than yourself. Seeing that there is something bigger than you puts life in better perspective. It helps you realize that you're not the center of the universe but rather you're a part of the whole. This is a freeing awareness and one that is very healthy for the soul.

When you volunteer, even though you are giving to another, you are also giving something positive and very important to yourself.

Stop and Reflect

Volunteer your way to less stress.

Circle the two types of volunteer work that most interest you. Working with:

Children

Victims of abuse

Elderly

Animals

Hands on work such as construction with Habitat for Humanity

Hospitals

Boys

Girls

Office work

Other? _____

Write down up to three volunteer opportunities you would be willing to pursue.

_____

_____

_____

Engage more frequently in your favorite hobby

What did you used to do before you had kids or before your present job? What used to challenge you in a positive way? What used to excite or motivate you? Whatever your answers, these are the things you need to do more of and are probably among your best flow experiences.

Answer the question I put forward earlier: On your deathbed how would you fill this in? I wish I had done more _____. Do this now. Don't wait.

Basically, any activity that takes your mind off stressful thinking can serve as a Stress Break and give you rest away from your stress. Do more of whatever activities you choose.

Stop and Reflect

Action Plan: Stress Breaks 1 to 8.

Check the following *Stress Breaks* you are willing to engage in regularly to release your stress energy:

_____Stress Break #1: Regular physical exercise (page 65)

_____Stress Break #2: Tense/relax muscles (page 71)

_____Stress Break #3: Laughter (page 72)

_____Stress Break #4: Journal (page 77)

_____Stress Break #5: Pleasure, passion and joy (page 80)

_____Stress Break #6: Friends (page 82)

_____Stress Break #7: Pursue "flow" activities (page 85)

_____Stress Break #8: Volunteer and hobbies (page 90)

Return to the corresponding pages and re-read the information for the *Stress Break(s)* you chose. On a separate sheet of paper write an action plan for each *Stress Break* you checked. Use the guidelines below to create your plan. Good luck!

- Write a specific goal you'll work toward to add to or increase this *Stress Break* in your life. Include how frequently you'll do something and when you'll start.

- Telling a trusted person about your intent increases the likelihood that you'll follow through. Who can you tell about your commitment?

- If you choose to do nothing when the time comes for you to begin using your **Stress Breaks**, say to yourself, ***"I choose to send cortisol coursing through my system."***

 ***"I choose to balance the cortisol in my body."***

Remember, it's a choice. You can choose to change or you can choose to stay the same.

CHAPTER 11

RELAX YOUR FIGHT/FLIGHT ENERGY

 *"I choose to balance
the cortisol in my body."*

THE OTHER WAY TO CHANNEL YOUR FIGHT/FLIGHT ENERGY in a healthy direction, and therefore decrease the excess cortisol coursing through your system, is to relax it. There is no good reason to go through day after day of crazy stress without also scheduling time for the relaxation response to counter the harmful effects of your possibly unhealthy lifestyle. If you choose to do nothing different then say, *"I choose to send cortisol coursing through my system."*

The more you balance stress with relaxation the more energy and the fewer conflicts you'll have. You'll sleep better and resist more illness and disease and you'll think more clearly. It sounds almost too good to be true. But it isn't. It's that simple!

Stress Break # 9: Deep breathe

Breathing is such a basic survival behavior that it seems odd that so many people don't do it correctly. With a typical workshop audience around 25% are not breathing correctly. With one particular audience of all CEOs about 80% weren't!

Breathing deeply is healthy. It helps center you physically, mentally and emotionally better than almost anything else. Deep breathing is instant stress reduction, so it's instantly self-calming and soothing. It can also increase your self-control when you're attempting to change any behavior.

Deep breathing is the physiological opposite of fight/flight breathing

When stressed your Stress Cycle, *SC*, as I call it, is triggered. This involves your thinking, emotions and your fight/flight response all of which trigger your reaction. The degree to which the *SC* is triggered is the degree to which you habitually, automatically, and defensively react. In other words, when your reaction is strongly defensive, when the *SC* is strongly engaged, you react as you always have; nothing changes.

Deep breathing is physiologically the opposite of the fight/flight breathing, which is more shallow and faster. Because deep breathing slows down the fight/flight response it decreases the amount of cortisol coursing through your body. It also slows down the *SC* so you can choose your response versus automatically and defensively reacting.

Once deep breathing centers you, you're more capable of making changes. For example, Fred, a coaching client, wanted to quit biting his fingernails. Each time he put his hand into his mouth he was instructed to take a slow deep breath. Then when he exhaled he was to imagine pushing away his hand. Repeating this over and over for a few weeks helped him break his habit.

Let's say you have a coworker you're tempted to punch, or a bully from whom you want to hide. Deep breathing can help you over-ride your fight/flight response. As you breathe deeply repeat your positive intent. "I'm interacting non-defensively with her." "I'm standing up for myself with him."

Do you breathe correctly?

When I teach participants in a stress workshop how to breathe properly I can generally tell who's not. They look like taking a deep breath is work, like it's a strain. Their eyes bug out a little and their upper chest and shoulders look stiff.

Have you ever checked to see if you breathe the way Mother Nature intends? Why not check it out right now? Stand and place one hand on your abdomen and the other on your chest. Take a couple of slow, deep breaths and notice which of your hands goes out more as you inhale. Try it now.

If your abdomen hand went out more as you inhaled, that's good, you're breathing properly.

If your chest hand went out more or if neither did that's not good. If so, try something else. Keep your hands in the same positions as you take a deep breath and then sigh very deeply pushing out the air completely. As you let the air back in notice again which hand goes out more. Many of those who had their chest hand or neither hand go out more the first time will notice their abdomen hand going out more.

If your chest still expands more when you inhale or if neither your chest nor your abdomen does, it probably means you don't exhale enough. When you exhale fully, your body tends to take over and do what it's supposed to do. Exhale longer than you inhale. Focus on exhaling more deeply for a few weeks until it becomes second nature.

Train yourself how to breathe correctly to avoid the shallow breathing symptoms. Assess your breathing as you sit and as you lie on your back. You're almost certainly breathing correctly and need to model it when you're standing. Maybe it's gravity that explains why you do it properly when sitting or lying down, I don't know. Become more conscious of your breathing to correct it.

Are you a chronic shallow breather?

Does it surprise you that the following symptoms can be caused by improper and shallow breathing?

- Headaches
- Muscle tension
- Exhaustion
- Anxiety
- Panic attacks
- Depression

If you have any of these symptoms quite regularly, part and perhaps all of your problem may be that you don't breathe properly or enough.

Chronic shallow breathing not only contributes to (if not causes) the above symptoms, it keeps you in a higher level of stress due to the increase of carbon dioxide in your blood. Wouldn't it be an easy fix to simply correct how you breathe? It's free and has no negative side effects. What a great deal!

I recommend this exercise for everyone who's stressed. Do it every hour on the hour for a week or two, or forever.

- Inhale slowly through your nose to the count of six (or eight whichever is better for you).
- Hold for the count of three (or four).
- Exhale slowly through your mouth to nine counts (or 12).
- Hold for three (or four).

Repeat for at least four rounds increasing to ten rounds.

If you get light-headed doing this four times while standing, you're almost certainly a shallow-chest breather. With practice you can retrain yourself to breathe properly.

Take the advice of Dr. Nick Hall, too. He advises not only the deep abdominal breathing but also deep breathing that expands the chest cavity. He recommends every other deep breath be abdominal with the next one expanding the chest.

Deep breathe to quit smoking

Deep breathing can even help you quit smoking! Smoking can be satisfying because as you inhale the smoke you are in essence deep breathing. Instead of grabbing for a cigarette, try deep breathing. Take it further as a friend of mine did when she quit. Sheila kept a cigarette pack full of straws cut to the same length as her cigarettes. Each time she wanted to smoke she pulled out one of the straws and deep breathed through it.

To sleep better

To relax or go to sleep, try deep breathing for a few minutes. With each breath notice how your body starts to relax and can reach that body sigh, a more complete letting go of tension. At this point you're likely to drift off to sleep or into the relaxed meditative state.

Calm yourself

Remember, deep breathing, which triggers the relaxation response, is the physiological opposite of fight/flight breathing. Precede any relaxation technique with a few minutes of deep breathing. Also, any time you want to calm down, deep breathe.

For example, if you're very nervous over an upcoming presentation, while you're rehearsing (you are rehearsing, right?) train yourself to take deep breaths occasionally. Not only will the centering help you think more clearly by slowing down your fight/flight response, it'll also fill your lungs with oxygen and steady your voice.

To get off to a good start, do as my soloist mother told me she did before each performance. As she approached the podium she took three deep breaths (not two, not four, but three) and rehearsed her opening passage in her mind. I adapted this to public speaking and it certainly helped me.

Replace stressful thoughts with goal attainment ones

Any time you have stressful thoughts in your head and they go on long enough, be very aware that you're sending cortisol coursing through your system. Take several deep breaths while replacing your stressful thoughts with thoughts that will lead you to whatever your positive goal is in your situation.

For example, one stress coaching client who frequently and defensively argued with her sister, wanted to change this pattern. She decided her new and positive goal was to find common ground with her sister; the opposite of the differences that one focuses on in times of conflict. Before they would get together for their weekly dinners she did deep breathing and said to herself, "I'm focusing on our common ground." While with her sister if she started to get defensive she'd instantly deep breathe and repeat her mantra over and over. With practice she was able to decrease her contribution to the tension and in response, little by little, her sister relaxed more and became defensive less often, too.

Get conscious

For deep breathing to help you in any of these situations, you must first truly want to be successful. You must also be conscious of when you need to deep breathe. If you're unaware that you bite your fingernails, or if you have no real desire to quit smoking, all the deep breathing in the world will do little good. Whatever behavior change you're committed to, deep breathing and the resulting centering are extremely helpful.

Diminish fatigue by breathing more and drinking more water

Recently I visited an old friend who told me that she loves my weekly published "Stress for Success" column and reads it every week. She chuckled and then said, "But I don't necessarily follow your advice." (Thanks, Elizabeth for keeping me grounded.)

I'm realistic enough to know that many of even the most stressed and exhausted among us, those who most need to faithfully practice stress reduction don't; many because they're just too tired. So here are two bits of advice that are easy to practice, they're free, require virtually no willpower or additional time, and yet still are very beneficial in boosting your energy:

- Breathe more deeply.
- Drink more water.

When you breathe shallowly, which stressed people do, you aren't taking in enough oxygen. With lower levels of oxygen and higher levels of carbon dioxide in your blood you become more tired and put pressure on your body because your heart rate and blood pressure go up.

So breathe deeply from your abdomen. Abdominal breathing gives an oxygen boost that energizes and relaxes you instantly. Do this before times you know you'll be stressed, like a difficult conversation you're about to have with someone.

Inhaling correctly (abdomen enlarges) expands your lower lungs allowing you to take in more air with each breath. Remember to concentrate on pushing the air out as you exhale, which encourages the body to breathe correctly. Maintaining good posture also facilitates healthy breathing.

Dehydration causes fatigue

It's estimated that 75% of Americans are chronically dehydrated. And no wonder! Look at all the caffeine we consume from coffee, tea and soda. And we simply don't drink enough water. If you're very stressed you're probably one of that dehydrated 75%. Besides fatigue, dehydration can cause headaches, constipation, and irritability.

"When you feel thirsty, you've already lost two to three percent of your body fluid" says Susan Kleiner, PhD RD, a registered dietician in Mercer Island, Washington. This can lower your blood volume, which means you don't get as much blood to your brain so your heart has to work harder.

Sometimes you mistakenly perceive your body's plea for water as hunger pains. For a few weeks when you think you're hungry between meals drink a glass of water instead. You'll hydrate yourself more and may decrease the extra pounds you put on over the years.

Also consider:

- Drinking enough water so you have to urinate once an hour during wakeful hours.

- Drinking decaffeinated herbal tea or soda, and eating more soup, fresh fruits and vegetables.

- Drinking lots of water in the morning when constipated. It works better than the over-the-counter products upon which we tend to rely.

- Avoiding drinks that contribute to dehydration such as coffee, tea, and alcoholic beverages, all of which are diuretics that require more water from the body than they provide.

- Having water nearby throughout your day, including in your car.

To generate more energy, which might motivate you to follow other needed stress management advice, breathe more deeply and drink more water. Do these two things regularly for the next two months and see if you're not more energetic. Then you'll have no excuse to stop you from taking better care of yourself in other ways.

Stress Break # 10: Deep relaxation

Along with regular physical exercise, practicing deep relaxation is the other most important *Stress Break* you can practice to balance the cortisol that courses through your system. Regular meditation promotes better moods, decreases muscle tension and stress, improves the immune system, and you'll probably sleep better at night due to a lower cortisol level.

Deep relaxation or meditation is a mental and physical state that is the opposite of the fight/flight response. So whereas under the fight/flight your body is on high alert pumping out hormones like cortisol, speeding up all of your physical systems needed for survival, relaxation brings about physical calmness and balance. This leads to mental and emotional tranquility and balance, as well.

Deep relaxation is extremely beneficial if you often experience (or even if you don't) these symptoms:

- Muscle tension
- Headaches and other physical problems
- Irritability and anxiety
- Frequent bouts of colds and flu
- Sleeplessness
- Difficulty focusing
- Lethargy
- Shallow breathing
- Panic attacks
- Any other frequent stress reaction

Researchers have long agreed upon the benefits of deep relaxation, including:

- Lowered blood pressure, respiration, and pulse rates.
- Release of muscle tension.
- Reduced emotional stress.
- Strengthening of the immune system.

Practicing regular deep relaxation several times a week, if not daily, greatly reduces stress, improves your thinking so you can be a more creative problem solver, and even slows down the aging process!

It's even more restorative than sleep. Herbert Benson, M.D., a pioneer in mind/body medicine, has defined the relaxation response and continues to lead teaching and research into its effectiveness in mitigating the harmful effects of stress. In his groundbreaking book, *The Relaxation Response* he reported that your mind and body slow down significantly more during relaxation than during sleep. When you sleep you use approximately 8% less oxygen than during wakefulness. When you're deeply relaxed you're using about 10–20% less oxygen.

Most people who meditate, myself included, will tell you that twenty minutes of deep relaxation is more or less equivalent to several hours of sleep! You'll still need the same amount of sleep at night that you've always needed since relaxation and sleep are different functions of the brain, but you'll feel much more refreshed and your body will be healthier if you add regular deep relaxation to your life.

What works?

What's relaxing for one may not be for another. Some of you may try relaxation and find yourself impatiently tapping your finger, wishing it to be over! You probably need it more than those who can easily and deeply relax.

Take heart, you can learn. The trick is to find a technique that works for you personally. It may take some of you longer to learn how to quiet your mind. To get going, just choose a technique that appeals to you while allowing your mind to tailor it to work better for you as time goes by.

In my stress reduction workshops I cover three different techniques to offer a choice, knowing that one will not suit all participants. Try one of these three ideas for the next few weeks.

- Prayer: some people become deeply relaxed when they pray. The real trick to deep relaxation is to focus intently on anything that relaxes you.

- Focus on your breathing: Dr. Benson recommends focusing on your inhale and as you exhale think of any short phrase or word that relaxes you, such as "I'm relaxed." That's all you need to do, over and over and over.

- Visualize a relaxing scene: your favorite vacation spot, the beach, the woods or incredible sunsets. Choose one scene and focus on what you would see, hear, feel and smell in this place.

For example, if you are imagining walking on the beach you would:

- See the water, the birds, clouds, waves, people, and plants.
- Hear some of these things.
- Smell the salt in the air, the fragrance of a flower.
- Feel the sun on your body, the sand between your toes.

Additional relaxation tips

- Set aside 20–30 minutes of uninterrupted time on a non-digesting stomach (before you eat a meal, not right after).
- Play relaxation music if you like. (Many different varieties are available from Whole Person Associates, www.wholeperson.com.)
- Sit upright with your spine straight with both feet on the floor. You can also lie down (don't fall asleep).
- Begin with deep breathing for a minute or two or until your body relaxes and sighs. Then, allow your breathing to return to normal and begin to focus on your chosen relaxation technique.
- It's perfectly normal for distracting thoughts to enter your mind. Do as Dr. Herbert Benson recommends, take another deep breath and think to yourself, "oh well," and return your breathing to normal and return to your relaxation technique. Or gently push away your distracting thoughts. Imagine pushing them to join other background thoughts that are circling above your head.
- Relax for 20 minutes (or work up to it). Set a quiet alarm for 25 minutes in case you don't come out of it on your own.
- Gently return your focus to the present and stretch before getting up.

Practice this powerful skill of deep relaxation regularly. Once you get good at it, I can almost promise you you'll find it to be one of the four most powerful stress reduction techniques (the others are regular exercise, humor and great problem solving).

Squeeze a few minutes of relaxation into each day

Far too many of us lead lives that are frenzied and hurried from the moment we wake up in the morning to the moment we crawl into bed at night. We are absolutely nuts!

The more packed every moment of your day is the more you need to make time to relax (rest); for a few minutes of deep breathing to 20 minutes of deep relaxation or yoga.

The human system can tolerate a tremendous amount of stress. Over the years, however, too much stress breaks down your resistance to illness and disease. Remember, the negative consequences of your stress are strongly influenced by your rest habits.

Since stress is unlikely to diminish in our high-pressured American lifestyle, throughout your day create time for the natural unwinding of your stress response.

You don't have time to rest, you say? You have more time than you think you do. You could:

- Do deep breathing while driving to work and during other stressful moments of your day.
- Get up 15 minutes earlier and spend the time doing deep relaxation, yoga or journaling.
- Take 2 minutes several times a day to tense tight muscle groups for 10 to 15 seconds, then relax them completely (see directions in Chapter 10).
- Use wind-down imaging before drifting off to sleep. Imagine yourself floating in the Caribbean off your favorite island (or whatever image relaxes you) for a few minutes as you slow down enough to fall asleep. If you use visualization for your deep relaxation, however, use a different one before sleeping. If you use the same one for relaxation that you use for sleep you'll just train yourself to fall asleep when you want to relax.
- Arrange quiet time at home where everyone honors a nonverbal sign on bedroom doors (like a hotel do not disturb sign) to give privacy. During this time you could do 30 minutes of exercise, deep relaxation or take a nap.

Don't wait for physical, emotional or mental symptoms to surface. Assume you would benefit from frequent *Stress Breaks* throughout your day. The more frantic your life, or the more chronic stress you're experiencing, the more rest you need to schedule to avoid damage to your physical, emotional and mental health. You'll be much more energetic, catch fewer colds and flus and protect your health for the short and the long run.

Stress Break #11: Human touch

We all know that humans need touch. Touching can reassure you, relax, comfort or arouse you like nothing else. We've all experienced moments when the touch of a trusted person's hand or a reassuring hug was all that was needed to reduce fear, anxiety, or loneliness. Touching is an act of connection, and humans need connection.

Research has shown:

- The amount of body contact infants receive plays a vital role in their mental and physical development.
- Touch is vital to the happiness of adults.
- Touch influences your ability to deal with discomfort and pain. For example, as a child with the flu I felt noticeably better when my mother sat with me and stroked my hair.
- Various studies have shown that when someone else gently holds a person's wrist, their heartbeat slows and blood pressure declines.
- Children and adolescents hospitalized for psychiatric problems show reductions in anxiety levels and positive changes in attitude after a brief daily back rub.

If you've traveled the world you've seen that different societies have very different attitudes toward touch. Interesting research from the 1960s studied the number of touches exchanged by pairs of people sitting in coffee shops around the world. In Puerto Rico people touched 180 times an hour, in Paris, 110 times an hour, in Gainesville, Florida, two times per hour, and in London, they never touched!

Unfortunately, not only are many of us less likely to touch, our increasingly hurried lifestyle combined with the fear of harassment lawsuits finds us touching less and less, leaving many touch-deprived. But the need for connection and close physical contact with others remains with you throughout your lifetime.

At least in your private life slow down and recommit to the importance of giving and receiving affection through positive touch. Satisfy this very basic need for yourself and your loved ones.

You can model affectionate behavior for your children. Make a concerted effort to touch your partner frequently throughout the day. Hug and kiss one another before you leave for work and when you return home. Hold hands during a movie and walking down the street.

When touching between two partners stops, it's a probable sign that the relationship is troubled. You may need to return to square one and discuss your individual needs for physical closeness. What are your likes and dislikes regarding touch? Taking the time to understand each other's preferences communicates love and respect. Honoring them will help you feel more connected and emotionally close, which builds trust.

Your kids also need the reassurance of touch. If they resist hugs, pat them on the back or tousle their hair. It's still touch. It's still connection. They feel more secure and loved when you greet them with affectionate touching. More importantly, they learn that they're loveable.

Take personal responsibility to get the touch you need. Express physical closeness with family and friends to improve your mood. If you've lost your spouse or if you're single and live alone, be sure to get your daily allotment of physical touch, even if that means through a massage or manicure.

Is there someone in a nursing home or a favorite niece or nephew you could show your affection to through positive touch? It's one of the greatest gifts you can give to yourself and to them.

Stress Break #12: Get enough sleep!

Sleep, glorious sleep. It's your reward after a hard day's work. There's much to be said for slipping into that deep and strange place. Restful sleep restores you fully so you can awaken the next morning refreshed and ready to take on another busy day.

Before Edison's invention of the light bulb Americans slept 10 hours a night! Imagine that! Today we average six hours and fifty-five minutes a night. The National Sleep Foundation recommends getting between seven and nine hours of sleep a night. One-third of us get less sleep than just five years ago.

According to the National Sleep Foundation, "As many as 47 million adults may be putting themselves at risk for injury, health and behavior problems because they aren't meeting their minimum sleep needs in order to be fully alert the next day." Also from the Sleep in America Poll:

- Almost 70% report frequent sleep problems; most have never been diagnosed.

- About 40 million suffer from chronic sleep disorders. Another 20–30 million experience intermittent sleep problems.
- Up to 47 million adults have less daytime productivity and may be putting themselves at risk for injury, health and behavior problems, accidents and illness and even early death.
- According to the Sleep America 2004 poll, 69% of children experience one or more sleep problems at least a few nights per week!
- Sleep problems are estimated to cost Americans $100 billion in lost productivity, medical expenses, sick leave, and personal and property damage.
- 51% of Americans reported that they drove while drowsy in the past year. Seventeen percent said they actually dozed off behind the wheel!

Only a minority of Americans get regular, good sleep. (No wonder there are so many cranky people around!) According to a Gallup Poll conducted for the NSF, almost 25% say that they have insomnia almost every night!

Lack of sleep also exacerbates whatever is stressing you. Conversely, enough sleep facilitates your physical, mental and emotional ability to combat stress.

Dr. Neil Kavey, the director of the Sleep Disorders Center at Columbia-Presbyterian Medical Center, finds that lack of sleep contributes to many serious health problems:

- Physical setbacks due to thyroid malfunction, insulin sensitivity and glucose metabolism, causing the secretion of the stress hormone, cortisol. (There it is again!)
- Cognitive and emotional problems.
- Increased irritability and other mood problems.
- Loss of concentration, alertness, judgment and the ability to perform tasks thus increasing the risk of accidents.
- Reduced quality of life and ill health.

How much sleep should you be getting?

It depends upon your age.

- Infants, 11–12 hours a night.
- Children and adults, eight or nine.
- Adolescents need as much sleep as younger children, a challenge with modern social and school schedules.
- Teenagers need a good 7.5 hours a night. If they don't get it regularly they're at greater risk than other groups when it comes to learning, mood, attitude and attention.
- Older people need as much sleep as other adults. They don't sleep as easily since they experience more sleep problems leading to the myth that our need for sleep decreases in later years.

Insomnia

Insomnia is not getting enough sleep due to problems falling asleep, staying asleep, trouble getting back to sleep once awakened or awakening too early. It's caused by physical and mental conditions as well as by stress. Virtually everyone is affected occasionally by it. Because it can become chronic, it's important to be diagnosed and treated if it persists for more than a month.

Symptoms of insomnia

- Irritability.
- Quarreling.
- Catching colds and flu.
- An accident looking for a place to happen.
- Seething in traffic jams.
- Overeating.
- Your head bobbing embarrassingly in meetings the next day.

These are some of the consequences for those who don't get enough regular sleep. Plus, inadequate amounts of sleep can also be aging you prematurely!

In the National Sleep Foundation 2007 poll, 60% of women reported good sleep a few nights a week, and 67% said they frequently experience sleep problems.

Is cortisol responsible for sleep problems, too?

Remember, part of cortisol's purpose is to help regulate your wake/sleep cycle. Cortisol levels peak around 6 a.m. to 8 a.m. to make you more alert to prepare you for the day ahead. Throughout the day cortisol gradually declines causing a drop in energy during mid-afternoon, slowing you down to prepare you to sleep when the sun goes down. (Yeah, like we go to sleep at 8:00 p.m.!)

But your modern lifestyle of carting your children to their respective activities, getting work done you've brought home or going to your many social activities, forces you to find ways to increase your energy later in the day. (Pass the caffeine!)

This is exactly what leads you to a state of too much activity and too little rest. You push yourself too hard to keep up with this crazy lifestyle using stimulants to keep going and denying your body and mind of required rest, which denies your elevated cortisol enough time to fully disperse.

So here you are at the end of another stressful day, trying to go to sleep but your eyes are wide open. Or you fall asleep quickly only to awaken at 3:00 a.m. and remain awake for hours. Why? Because too much stress has sent too much cortisol coursing through your system throughout the day and into the night! And cortisol makes you more alert! Get it?

Sleep is more important to a healthy lifestyle than you may realize. The longer you go with mediocre sleep the more it will negatively affect your overall mental and physical health. Nothing else will improve significantly without better rest, especially if the sleep problem is chronic.

Rather than automatically reaching for a sleeping pill, pursue the following ideas to help you find a real solution to what's keeping you awake, not just a band-aid to temporarily mitigate the problem.

The solution is more regular sleep (duh!)

This is, of course, easier said than done: the more stressed you are the more you'll experience elevated cortisol levels at night, so the less likely you are to sleep. It's a vicious cycle.

The advice to help you sleep better is not surprisingly the same as reducing your overall stress:

- Exercise regularly. A sedentary lifestyle is a major contributor to sleeplessness.
- Close to bedtime do something easy like take a walk or do yoga.
- Avoid a large meal, vigorous exercise, nicotine and alcohol close to bedtime.
- Do daily meditation at least a few hours before bedtime.
- Avoid excessive napping.
- Maintain a regular sleep schedule, even on the weekends if you have trouble sleeping regularly.
- Journal your worries before bedtime.
- Choose a relaxing bedtime ritual like a warm bath or reading.
- Obviously, avoid caffeine in any form (coffee, tea, soda, chocolate). It's one of the greatest inhibitors of sleep. Caffeine rids your body of B-vitamins, the nutrients that keep you calmer, too.
- If you can't sleep, get up and read until you feel sleepy, then return to bed. This helps to reset your sleep clock.
- Chamomile tea may help.
- Medications (anti-depressants, blood pressure, heart and anti-seizure) may be keeping you awake. Talk to your physician about alternative treatments.
- Don't try so hard. Do you check the clock during the night to see how much sleep you're missing? This disturbs sleep! Set an alarm and put it out of reach and sight and don't let your mind go there.
- My husband allows himself to think about only one thing when he has trouble sleeping. Soon he drifts off.

Make it darker

Become more aware of how light and dark affect your sleep. Strong light or sunlight is the most powerful regulator of your biological clock that influences when you feel alert or sleepy.

If you wake up too early in the morning increase your exposure to bright light in the evening by an hour or two. During the winter use a light box or light visor, found in specialty stores. This may be particularly helpful for the elderly.

Wear an eye mask. To sleep beyond dawn, I wear my comfy eye mask and can do something I stopped doing a decade ago—sleep as late as I want. If you have persistent trouble sleeping, however, be careful about sleeping in. It would be better for you to have a very regular sleep and wake schedule, even on the weekends. The luxury of sleeping late on a weekend morning is great, but not if you find yourself counting sheep Sunday evening.

Light blocking shades: spend the money if your sleep is bad enough to justify it.

Consult a sleep specialist to determine whether changing your exposure to light could improve your sleep.

Decrease the noise

Noise is another obvious sleep inhibitor. How much traffic noise is around you? Noises inside your home like a sleeping partner who snores or animals making noises can make sleep difficult. Older people can be more bothered by noise if their sleep is more easily disrupted. Try these ideas to limit noise:

- Earplugs. These are a must for me when I'm sleeping in a noisy hotel. They push away distracting noise as if it were in a tunnel down the hallway.
- White noise from a water fountain, noise machine or fan.
- Good acoustics (rugs, heavy curtains) in your bedroom to absorb noise, especially sharp noises.
- Double-pane windows to cut down on external noise.
- Relaxing music or environmental sounds on a machine that plays for however long you program it.

To nap or not to nap, that is a good question

If you nap during the day to make up for the sleep you're not getting at night it could increase your insomnia. The research differs on whether or not naps facilitate nighttime sleep. Experiment. For a week take no naps and see if your nighttime sleep improves. If there is no difference, decrease the number and length of your naps over a longer period of time to see if there is any positive effect on nighttime sleep.

The sleep tips listed above may not be enough for those who suffer from sleep disorders such as sleep apnea, narcolepsy, and restless legs. If you have chronic sleep disorders consult your physician or a reputable sleep clinic for recommended treatment.

Sleep apnea

Snoring loudly at night, being sleepy during the daytime, and/or experiencing frequent long pauses in breathing while asleep followed by choking and gasping for breath are symptoms of the common and serious disorder sleep apnea. It affects as many as 18 million people according to the National Institute of Health. Daytime performance may be seriously affected and it can also lead to hypertension, heart disease, heart attack and stroke. The good news is this can be treated so you can live a normal life.

Narcolepsy

Narcolepsy is a particularly frustrating condition that finds a sufferer falling asleep uncontrollably anytime, anywhere even after a great night's sleep. According to the Narcolepsy Network it's a chronic neurological disorder that involves the body's nervous system and affects approximately 293,000 Americans. Sufferers also experience daytime sleepiness, muscle weakness or even paralysis, and disrupted nighttime sleep. There are medications and other treatments that can help control the symptoms although there is no known cure.

Restless legs syndrome (RLS)

Restless legs syndrome, affecting up to 12 million Americans, is experienced as a tingling sensation in the legs and perhaps the arms while sitting or lying still, especially at bedtime. Attempts to relieve these uncomfortable and sometimes painful symptoms by constantly stretching create a problem falling or staying asleep. People with restless legs usually feel extremely sleepy and function at a lower level during the day. Good sleep habits and medication can help someone with RLS.

If your sleep problem persists, talk with your doctor to see if there is an unknown cause that can be treated. To get more information on these and other sleep problems contact the National Sleep Foundation at www. sleepfoundation.org.

To keep up with your probable crazy American schedule you simply must get enough good sleep or you'll suffer consequences that compound your stress. I've known people who've suffered sleep problems over a long period of time and who subsequently experienced significant physical and mental health problems. Do whatever you need to do to get regular good sleep and you'll find the rest of your stress becomes more manageable.

Stop and Reflect

Get better sleep.

Are you getting enough sleep?

- Infants, 11–12 hours a night.
- Children to all adults, eight or nine.

Which insomnia symptoms do you experience?

_____ Problems falling asleep.

_____ Trouble staying asleep.

_____ Trouble getting back to sleep once awakened.

_____ Awakening too early.

Which of the following are you willing to explore as a possible, partial solution to improve your sleep?

_____ Exercise regularly, remembering that if you workout close to bedtime do something easy like a walk or yoga.

_____ Avoid large meals, vigorous exercise, nicotine and alcohol close to bedtime.

_____ Meditate daily, a few hours before bedtime.

_____ Avoid excessive napping.

_____ Maintain a regular sleep schedule, even on the weekends.

_____ Journal your worries before bedtime.

_____ Establish a relaxing bedtime ritual like a warm bath or reading.

_____ Avoid caffeine in any form (coffee, tea, soda, chocolate).

_____ To reset your sleep clock when you can't sleep, get out of bed and read something soothing until you feel sleepy; then return to bed.

_____ Drink a cup of chamomile tea.

_____ Talk to your physician. If your medications might be keeping you awake, discuss alternatives.

_____ Make it darker in your bedroom (see page 111).

_____ If waking up too early, increase exposure to bright light the evening before:

- Wear an eye mask.
- Light blocking shades.

_____ Consult a sleep specialist.

_____ Stop or decrease daytime napping.

_____ Change the ambient noise:

- Earplugs.
- White noise from a water fountain, noise machine or fan.
- Install rugs or heavy drapes.
- Install double-pane windows to deaden the noise from outside.
- Play relaxing music or environmental sounds.

_____ Other:

- Don't try so hard.
- Stop checking the clock.
- Focus your thinking on one pleasant thought.

Chapter 12

Panic Attacks and the Fight/flight

A feeling of imminent danger and loss of control, an intense desire to escape throwing you into a state of panic, accompanied by chest pain, heart palpitations, shortness of breath, dizziness, nausea or stomach discomfort and muscle tension might be a panic attack.

When you have panic attacks you know intimately how they feel: your life changes. You experience intense anxiety between episodes and avoid the situations and places that trigger them. Your world shrinks.

A panic attack is defined as the abrupt onset of an episode of intense fear or discomfort, which peaks in about 10 minutes. Many suffer from them without ever having been diagnosed. Because the symptoms mimic physical ailments, much time and money is spent on medical diagnostic tests that often turn up no physical cause. As the symptoms continue, so too does the worry that another panic attack will strike so the search for a physical cause, therefore solution continues.

The Anxiety Disorders Association of America reports an estimated 40 million Americans suffer from anxiety disorders. This disorder appears before age 24 for about half the sufferers. Women are twice as likely as men to develop it. (Since shallow breathing is part of panic attacks could it be that far more women suffer from them because they're more likely to breathe shallowly due to the socialization to have flat stomachs?)

While panic can happen because of an actual traumatic experience, in other situations it doesn't matter whether the threat is real. Often, panic happens after several weeks or months of stress. It happens more often to people who worry excessively, perfectionists, those who are socially avoidant or who experienced childhood abuse.

Possible symptoms of panic attacks

- Sweating
- Trembling
- Choking
- Racing heartbeat
- A smothering feeling
- Tingling in fingers and toes
- Can't get enough air
- Hot flashes or sudden chills
- Paralyzing terror
- Fear of dying or going crazy
- Things seem unreal, depersonalization

No wonder so many who panic think they have a serious physical illness and go from doctor to doctor as symptoms shift. The symptoms can mimic a variety of ailments so an accurate diagnosis is often not made until extensive medical testing fails to diagnose anything physical. Sufferers are often tested for hypoglycemia, heart arrhythmia and hyperventilation syndrome, angina, asthma, irritable bowel syndrome, colitis, vertigo, mitral valve prolapse, hypertension, or hiatal hernia.

Misdiagnosis and treatment of anxiety disorders costs billions annually, according to "The Economic Burden of Anxiety Disorders" study published in the Journal of Clinical Psychiatry.

- More than $42 billion/year, almost 1/3 of the total mental health bill for the U. S.
- Almost $23 billion for the repeated use of health care services, as sufferers seek relief from their assumed physical ailments.
- People who panic are three-to-five times more likely to go to the doctor and six times more likely to be hospitalized for psychiatric disorders than non-suffers.

Consequences of untreated panic attacks

After experiencing panic attacks approximately 10% become housebound and may even develop agoraphobia, the fear of open spaces. For many, agoraphobia can spread to other situations and locations shrinking the sufferer's world even more. Some eventually cut themselves off from almost everything. If panic attacks continue some will even lose their jobs and can be at greater risk for alcoholism not to mention depression. Clients I have worked with also tend to have marital problems.

It's the fight/flight response!

When I teach panic attack treatment classes, participants are relieved to find out that panic attacks are simply the normal fight/flight response in the extreme (although there is too high a production of the epinephrine and norephinephrine versus the cortocorticoids.) Everything covered so far in this book about the stress response and the cortisol coursing through your system applies to panic attacks as well.

There is much scientific research going on to identify the causes. It's believed that heredity plays a role as does catastrophic thinking, which exaggerates the normal stress response. In fact, when panic strikes, it bypasses the rational thinking part of the brain and keeps you in the amygdala, the area of the brain responsible for vigilance, including the fear response. Daniel Goleman, author of the best-selling book, *Emotional Intelligence*, calls the panic response emotional hijacking. It's virtually impossible to think rationally when trapped in the amygdala.

Panic attacks are largely driven by beliefs (thoughts)

The immediate cause of panic attacks is the belief that you're trapped or helpless, whether accurate or not. Worrying excessively about the attacks and obsessively avoiding situations that seem to bring on the panic are what perpetuate them. Here are some of the most common beliefs (thoughts) that trigger panic, which find a person catastrophically misinterpreting the meaning of physical symptoms.

The fight/flight symptoms of your attacks are closely linked to the type of thoughts you have. Here are some examples:

- Fear of a physical disaster leads to a racing heart, shortness of breath, dizziness, etc.

  "I'm having a heart attack." A panic attack may feel like a heart attack but your heart is designed to react this way when your mind perceives extreme threat. Unless you have cardiovascular problems, your heart's intense workout during a panic attack is unlikely to hurt you. Check with your doctor to make absolutely sure your heart is fine.

  "I can't breathe" or "I'm going to pass out!" Fight/flight breathing is faster and shallower so you are actually taking in more air, not less.

The shortness of breath you may feel is due to hyperventilation. Any light-headedness can be caused by too much carbon dioxide from too much hyperventilation.

- Fear of a psychological disaster like losing control or going crazy leads to feelings of a loss of reality.

"I'm going crazy!" or "I'm losing control!" Because the fight/flight, especially in the extreme bypasses the rational part of your brain, it's common that you could feel out of control. This can trigger all kinds of fearful and irrational thoughts, one of which is the fear of going crazy.

"I'm going to do something embarrassing!" Most people keep their panic to themselves so others are unlikely to even notice that you're going through something. And even if they do, what's the worst outcome? Remind yourself that panic attacks generally last for only a few minutes so if you can just hold on for awhile longer you'll likely come out of it and return to more of a semblance of physical and emotional balance. Do not exacerbate the power of panic over you by thinking panicky thoughts during the physical symptoms nor after they subside.

Take control of your catastrophic thinking. Whatever the nature of your fearful thinking ask the following questions:

- What's the worst thing that could happen in this situation?
- Have I ever experienced consequences as serious as I have imagined?
- Even if the worst happens, how important will it be in one year?

Learn to challenge fearful beliefs that are triggering your panic attacks such as:

Catastrophic thought: "I'll go crazy if I get stuck in an elevator!"

Rational response: Everyone who gets stuck in elevators eventually gets out. I've never heard of anyone dying from being stuck in one. Even if I were to get trapped, it would only last a relatively short period of time. It may prove uncomfortable but eventually I would get out and I would return to normal. Besides, maybe I would meet someone interesting on the elevator.

Hyperventilation (over breathing)

Most panic attacks are accompanied by hyperventilation. Ironically the reason you hyperventilate is because you think you don't have enough oxygen when the opposite is actually true; hyperventilation is a symptom of too much oxygen!

Symptoms of hyperventilation

• Light-headedness	• Shortness of breath	• Numbness
• Heart palpitations	• Chest pains	• Dizziness
• Sweating	• Tremors	• Weakness/fatigue
• Dry mouth	• Difficulty swallowing	• Clammy hands

Back in the 1970s during my Peace Corps stint in Colombia, South America, I had a panic attack when on a frighteningly over-packed, bald-tired, little bus (*buseta*) made for 12 people, while flying down the immense Andes Mountains in Bolivia.

There were 19 of us packed in with everyone's luggage crammed into every available nook and cranny. I started to panic! My mind raced with thoughts like, "Oh my god! We're going to have an accident! With all of these people on this bus I know I'll get trampled! I won't be able to get off!"

Phew! What a panic I worked myself into. Panic attack symptoms were flying through my mind and body!

I found myself deep breathing and calming my thoughts. I assessed my options (go nuts, calm down or tell the driver to stop and let me off in the middle of nowhere). Gratefully my panic subsided.

Since then, I've pushed any hint of panic away by breathing deeply and thinking calming or in control thoughts.

This failed to work for me, however, when I was going through the incredible stress of my parents' end-of-life illnesses.

I've already noted that my stress was exceedingly high during the 1½ years of caregiving. Toward the end of this time I began to experience panic attacks when driving over high bridges (lucky me, I live in coastal Florida!). I did what I'd done before to limit a panic attack plus more that

I've learned since my Peace Corps days: deep abdominal breathing with an extra focus on a longer exhale than inhale (Chapter 11) and tighten muscle groups then release them (Chapter 10). I'm sure this helped but not enough.

So I did more research on panic attacks to educate myself further. I discovered that I was breathing too frequently; around 25 or more inhales a minute. According to the Weill Cornell Medical College of Cornell University respiration rates while at rest should range from 15–20 per minute. Anything over 25 or fewer than 12 breaths per minute while resting could be considered abnormal. So I monitored my breathing to keep it within the normal range. Over time it helped me to get rid of the obsessive self-awareness I had developed of my extremely shallow breathing, which contributed to the reemergence of my panic attacks.

Minimize hyperventilation

Anyone who has experienced many panic attacks realizes how aware you become of your own breathing. The thought of learning to breathe more evenly and normally seems difficult. At least it did to me.

If you hyperventilate you will almost certainly experience the symptoms of panic. The trick is to learn to breathe more evenly and naturally. Here's some advice that works:

- Hold your breath for between 10 and 15 seconds, repeating a few times. This can calm hyperventilation quickly for some people.
- Breathe in and out of a paper bag, allowing you to re-inhale the carbon dioxide that you've exhaled. This improves your oxygen/carbon dioxide balance so you can more efficiently use the excess oxygen in your system.
- Vigorously exercise while breathing in and out through your nose. This also counters hyperventilation. Regular exercise also decreases your overall stress level, which keeps you out of the higher stress zone, which can push you into panic attack range.
- Exercising is the best way to regulate your breathing if it tends to be too shallow or irregular (too much breathing or too little). As always, check with your doctor before beginning an exercise program.
- Do abdominal breathing as described in Chapter 11. Inhale to the count of eight and exhale to the count of 12 (or 6/9). Exhale more

than you inhale to decrease your anxiety level. The more regularly you practice this breathing pattern the easier it will be to call upon the relaxation response during a panic producing situation, making it more difficult to panic.

Other ways to calm down your panic attacks

Many people who experience panic are successfully treated with antidepressants and/or anti-anxiety drugs. However, before relying upon prescription medication you might want to try the following techniques.

- Move from the emotional to the thinking part of your brain, the neocortex: give your rational brain an assignment to rate the intensity of your panic on a scale of one (low panic) to 10 (extreme panic). As your panic symptoms ebb and flow, continue to calibrate them, which puts you more into rational thinking versus being at the mercy of your amygdala.

- Desensitization: Panic attacks basically work through the unconscious part of your mind. Without you consciously realizing it, when your unconscious perceives a situation in which you have panicked before it tends to trigger panic again. You associate that situation or place with panic so you avoid it in the future to avoid panicking. But avoiding your supposed triggers feeds your fear. Instead, you need to desensitize yourself to those places and situations. Search for a skilled therapist who can lead you through visualization exercises to break the association between these places and situations and panic.

- Self-help materials. Try prepared materials such as Whole Person Associates' *9-Week Recovery Program* by Shirley Babior and Carol Goldman (www.wholeperson.com).

- "Be Aware of Panic Attacks" is an approach by Dr. Mark Eisenstadt, M.D., a British psychiatrist who has worked with these issues for over 30 years. His web site at http://www.phobics-Awareness.org is full of great materials. He suggests that being A-W-A-R-E helps:

    Accept the anxiety rather than fight it. Getting scared, angry or fighting the anxiety simply makes it worse. Remember, a panic attack is simply the fight/flight, a natural physiological reaction to stress, only to the extreme. It won't kill you nor make you crazy.

Watch your anxiety. Don't judge it as bad, it just is, at least for now. Remember, that it will pass in a few short minutes.

Act normally. Even though your impulse is to try to escape the situation you believe is triggering your panic go about your business as you intended before the panic attack hit. This also begins to program your brain to realize that the situation is really not a threat to you. Do the 8/12 breathing.

Repeat the steps. Continue to accept the anxiety, watch it and act normally until it passes.

Expect the best. Whatever it is that you fear, for instance having a heart attack, will probably not even come close to happening. After your panic subsides you will be in the same condition you were before it began.

Practicing these techniques can over time reduce your panic attacks so that they become much more manageable. Ultimately, however, to do away with panic attacks once and for all, you will need to reduce your overall stress. Keep yourself out of that heightened stress zone where panic attacks are more likely to strike you.

Seek out professional help. Effective therapy can help 70% to 90% of the people who seek help to reduce if not prevent panic attacks. These therapists use a variety of techniques, such as:

- Cognitive-behavioral Therapy: Since distorted thinking is the cause of most panic attacks this approach helps you to recognize and change the irrational thought patterns that lead to panic. Basically, you would learn to move yourself away from the fearful thinking to something that is more rational.

- Since deep relaxation (see Chapter 11) is the physiological opposite of the fight/flight it is one of the most important techniques to practice regularly. When you get skilled at deeply relaxing you can call upon that feeling when stressed. Do the 8/12 breathing, which automatically slows down the fight/flight and follow that with recalling the deep sense of relaxation that you have learned to achieve during meditation.

- Pair a pleasing fragrance, like lavender, with a peaceful meditation. After a few sessions, the odor itself will trigger a relaxed state, even when you're not meditating. Use that fragrance when you feel panicky.

- Follow the breathing with the tensing of muscle groups for 10 to 15 seconds and then relaxing (Chapter 10). The breathing exercise relaxes the fight/flight energy and the muscle tensing followed by relaxing releases it.

There is no reason why you should have to suffer from panic attacks. They are relatively easy to successfully treat. Consider seeing a qualified therapist. Since information is power, research panic attacks, including through the Anxiety Disorders Association of America at http://www.adaa.org.

CHAPTER 13

DEVELOP MENTAL STRATEGIES TO STOP UNPRODUCTIVE REACTIONS

TRYING TO CHANGE ANY BEHAVIOR can itself be stressful, not to mention difficult. Part of the reason for the difficulty is that when you're stressed, your *Stress Cycle* is triggered and it speeds up your reaction time. The fight/flight, given that it is energy being triggered, is what largely pushes you to respond automatically as you always have in similar situations. The more stressed you are the faster you're likely to react.

Creating a *Space of Time* between the stressful event and your reaction to it allows you to respond differently. It gives you a millisecond to discipline yourself to change from your typical and unproductive reaction to something more effective.

Use *Mental Strategies* to create this *Space of Time*. What I mean by *Mental Strategies* is to play a little game inside your own head to stop your own automatic and ineffectual reactions.

Mental Strategies don't solve problems. Their intended purpose is to give you the power to change. Here are some examples.

Deep breathing can help you make behavioral changes. Instead of reacting emotionally to someone you normally find aggravating, immediately upon perceiving your stress, take a deep breath or two to slow down your defensive reaction.

Mental Strategies work best when you personalize them to your situation. For example, a nurse was very intimidated by a physician who frequently yelled at her. She'd quake in his presence and tolerate his berating behavior. One day as he was yelling at her she found herself focusing on his moustache and fantasized about it growing and growing. She began to use this as a *Mental Strategy* sometimes decoratively arranging mustache curly-cues around his face. On days when she was in a foul mood she'd imagine the long mustache choking him. Not long after she started this little game he stopped yelling at her. I bet he picked up on her changed nonverbal cues. The corners of her mouth probably turned up almost imperceptibly and he began to perceive her as no longer intimidated therefore, no longer an easy target.

When my older stepson moved in with us I found myself being overly critical of him. I hated this reaction in me but he would do something and I would automatically pounce. I tried deep breathing, looking for humor in the situation but nothing worked well. One day as I was about to criticize him, an image popped into my mind that worked as a *Mental Strategy* from that day on—most of the time anyway. I pictured my mother and father watching their dear sweet daughter being so hard on this child. That's all I needed. It stopped me in my tracks. It created a *Space of Time* so I could walk away from the situation.

A last example is of a young boy who told his father that he feared being alone in his bedroom at night. His father taught him to hum the song, *When the Saints Come Marching In*, whenever he became scared. It pushed away his fears and allowed him to fall asleep sooner.

Affirmations can help you create a *Space of Time*, as well. Decide how you want to be in order to overcome your typical, unproductive reaction. For example, if you easily lose your cool with someone in your life and you want to change that, how would you need to be in order to not lose your cool? Calm? Composed? Focused? Assertive? Choose one to four ways you would need to be and create an affirmation:

"I'm calm and assertive."

Repeat this affirmation to yourself dozens of times. Increase how often you repeat it during the times you will be with this person. Eventually the use of this mantra can create that *Space of Time* for you to react the way you want.

Mental Strategies that can work for you are limited only by your own creativity. Come up with some image, thought, humor or just use deep breathing to stop unproductive reactions. Create a *Space of Time* to increase your opportunity for change.

Be patient because this, like anything, takes time. Plus it doesn't always work. If it can increase your success rate at stopping undesirable behavior even a little, it'll be worth the effort. Learn this skill well and you'll find your success rate soaring.

Stop and Reflect

Action plan: Chapters 11 to 13.

Check the following *Stress Breaks* you are willing to engage in regularly to release your stress energy:

_____ Chapter 11: Relax your fight/flight energy (page 95)

_____ Stress Break #9: Deep breathe (page 95)

_____ Stress Break #10: Deep relaxation (page 101)

_____ Stress Break #11: Human touch (page 105)

_____ Stress Break #12: Sleep (page 107)

_____ Chapter 12: Panic Attacks and the fight/flight (page 116)

_____ Chapter 13: Develop *Mental Strategies* (page 125)

Return to the corresponding pages and re-read the information for the *Stress Break(s)* you chose. On a separate sheet of paper write an action plan for each *Stress Break* you checked. Use the guidelines below to create your plan. Good luck!

- Write a specific goal you'll work toward to add to or increase this *Stress Break* in your life. Include how frequently you'll do something and when you'll start.

- Telling a trusted person about your intent increases the likelihood that you'll follow through. Who can you tell about your commitment?

- If you choose to do nothing when the time comes for you to begin, say to yourself,

 *"I choose to send cortisol coursing through my system."*

Remember, it's a choice. You can focus on the healthier pledge:

 *"I choose to balance
the cortisol in my body."*

And let it motivate you to make healthy changes.

CHAPTER 14

THE BALL'S IN YOUR COURT

I'VE DONE MY BEST to get you to wake up to the harm stress is doing to you and hope I have inspired you to want to take responsibility by getting yourself into better *Stress Shape*. Most of us know what we should do, whether or not we do it. It's the why we need to change habits that most seem to not fully understand.

Stated one more time, it's largely the cortisol that's released into our bodies too often and for too long when stressed that is making us sick and killing us prematurely.

Take responsibility for your own health and practice the easy part of stress management by adding daily *Stress Breaks* to mitigate this damage—or at least remain conscious that you choose to not protect yourself.

The ball is in your court, where it belongs and frankly, where it always has been. Only you can be responsible for you.

Finally, I hope you will say less often, *"I choose to send cortisol coursing through my system,"* and replace it with

 *"I choose to balance the cortisol in my body."*

♫ *Slow Down* [because] *You Move Too Fast!* ♫ And keep breathing!

REFERENCES

Benson, Herbert. Klipper, Miriam. 1975. The Relaxation Response. HarperCollins Publishing. New York.

Brief overview of anxiety disorders. Anxiety Disorders Association of America: http://www.adaa.org/GettingHelp/Briefoverview.asp.

Cacioppo, John T. Visser, P. S., & Pickett, C. L. (2005). *Social neuroscience: People Thinking About Thinking People.* Cambridge, MIT Press.

Cederquist, Caroline. 2008. "Health Column". *News Blaze*, Naples, FL. www.newsblaze.com/health.

Chrousos, George, Gold, Phillip, Goodwin, F.K. 1988. "Clinical and Biochemical Manifestionations of Depression." *New England Journal of Medicine.* Vol. 319:413-420. August 18, 1988. No. 7.

Csikszentmihalyi, Mihaly. 1990. Flow: *The Psychology of the Optimum Experience.* Harper and Row. New York.

Development and Psychopathology. 2006. 173-194 Cambridge University Press Copyright © 2006 Cambridge University Press doi:10.1017/S095457940606010X Published online by Cambridge University Press 10 Feb 2006: http://journals.cambridge.org/action/displayAbstract?fromPage=online&aid=405287.

DiLorenzo, Terry, et al. "A Model of Disease-Specific Worry in Heritable Disease". *Journal of Behavioral Medicine*, Vol. 29, No. 1.

Goleman, Daniel. 1997. *Emotional Intelligence.* Bantam Books. New York.

Hall, Nick. 2007. "Emotion, Stress and Disease". Institute for Natural Resources. Concord, CA.

Hall, Nick. Spring, 2008. "Self-destructive Emotions". The Institute for Brain Potential.

Hodgson, Harriet. 2005. "Don't Be a Worry Wort". Ezine. http://EzineArticles.com/?expert=Harriet_Hodgson.

Huton, Mark. 2008. "Regular and Occassional Volunteers: How and Why They Help Out". *Institute for Volunteering Reaserch: Research Bulletins.* http://www.ivr.org.uk/researchbulletins.

Jeffers, D. S. (1987). *Feel the Fear and Do It Anyway.* NY, NY: Ballantine Books.

Kavey, Neil. 2005. "Less Sleep Could Mean Less Sex". http://www.cbsnews.com/stories/2005/03/29/earlyshow/health/main683649.shtml.

Kessler, Ronald C., Greenberg, Paul E. "The Economic Burden of Anxiety and Stress Disorders". http://www.acnp.org/asset.

Kleiner, Susan. June 19, 2006. "Drinking water for health." Retrieved December 23, 2008, from Web MD: http://www.webmd.com/food-recipes/features/feel-your-best-with-water.

Lee Berk, D. http://www.llu.edu/llu/faculty/directory/portfolio_activity.php?uid=lberk&catid=8.

Martin, J. P. (2008). "What Do Happy People Do?" *Social Indicators Research.* http://www.springerlink.com/content/t482u48402883086.

Merz, Noel Bairey. April 2007. *US News and World Report.*

Miller, Michael. University of Maryland Medical Center: http://www.umm.edu/features/laughter.htm.

Outwardly Expressed Anger Affects Some Women's Heart Arteries. Retrieved October 17, 2008, from Science Daily: http://www.sciencedaily.com/releases/2007/01/070114185909.htm.

Pamela Peek, M. M. 2001. *Fight Fat after Forty.* Penguin Books. New York.

Perfetti, Richardo, M. D. Retrieved October 2, 2008, from Cedars Sinai Medical Center: http://www.cedars-sinai.edu/5228.html.

Poll, N. S. 2007. *Sleep in America Polls.* National Sleep Foundation: http://www.sleepfoundation.org/site/c.huIXKjM0IxF/b.2417353/k.6764/Sleep_in_America_Polls.htm.

Sapolsky, Robert M. 1995, 1998, 2004. *Why Zebras Don't Get Ulcers.* NY, NY: Henry Holt & Company, LLC.

Seligman, D. M. 1991. *Learned Optimism.* Pocket Books. New York.

Seligman, D. M. *Authentic Happiness: Using the New Positive Psychology.* University of Pennsylvania Authentic Happiness: http://www.authentichappiness.sas.upenn.edu/Default.aspx.

Shawn Talbott, P. 2002. *The Cortisol Connection Why Stress Makes You Fat and Ruins Your Health.* Hunter House, Inc. Alameda, California.

Shute, Nancy April 23, 2007. "Over the Limit". *US News and World Report.*

Stroke: Hope Through Research. Oct. 15, 2008. National Institute of Nuerological Disorders and Stroke: http://www.ninds.nih.gov/disorders/stroke/detail_stroke.htm#124361105.

Talbot, Shawn. 2007. The Cortisol Connection: *Why Stress Makes You Fat and Ruins Your Health—And What You Can Do about It.* Alameda, CA. Hunter House.

Taylor, Shirley. 13 Dec. 2006. "Tend and Befriend" Current Directions in Psychological Science. Vol. 15, Issue 6, pp 273-277.

Zeratsky, Katherine. February 28, 2008. *Tools for healthier lives.* http://www.mayoclinic.com/health/cortisol-blockers/AN01275.

Helpful Web Sites

American Institute of Stress: www.stress.org/Effects_of_stress.htm.

Anxiety Disorders Association of America: http://www.adaa.org.

WebMD.com. www.webmd.com.

Narcolepsy Network: Benefits and services for Narcoleptics and their families. http://www.narcolepsynetwork.org.

National Institute of Health: www.nih.gov.

National Sleep Foundation: http://www.sleepfoundation.org/site/c.huIXKjM0IxF/ b.2417141/k.27D9/Home_of_the_Sleep_in_America_Poll.htm.

Mayo Clinic.www.mayoclinic.com/health/cortisol-blockers.

Science Daily: http://www.sciencedaily.com/releases/2007/01/070114185909.htm.

American Institute of Stress (The), University of Maryland http://www.stress.org/Effects_of_stress.htm.

31901046515690

LaVergne, TN USA
04 December 2009
165912LV00013B/38/P